MILLIONAIRE UPGRADE

Lessons in success from those who travel at the sharp end of the plane

RICHARD PARKES CORDOCK

CAPSTONE

First published 2006 by
Capstone Publishing Limited (a Wiley Company)
The Atrium
Southern Gate
Chichester
West Sussex
PO19 8SQ
www.wileyeurope.com
Email (for orders and customer service enquires): cs-books@wiley.co.uk

Reprinted February 2006

CIP catalogue records for this book are available from the British Library and the US Library of Congress

ISBN 13:   978-1-84112-703-3 (PB)
ISBN 10:   1-84112-703-5 (PB)

Typeset in Swiss 11/16pt by Sparks Computer Solutions, Oxford (www.sparks.co.uk)

Printed and bound in Great Britain by TJ International Ltd, Padstow, Cornwall
This book is printed on acid-free paper responsibly manufactured from sustainable forestry in which at least two trees are planted for each one used for paper production.

Substantial discounts on bulk quantities of Capstone Books are available to corporations, professional associations and other organizations. For details telephone John Wiley & Sons on (+44) 1243-770441, fax (+44) 1243 770571 or email corporatedevelopment@ wiley.co.uk

ENDORSEMENTS FOR *MILLIONAIRE UPGRADE*

'It took me a long time to learn this stuff – I wish I'd been on that plane 30 years ago!'
Simon Woodroffe – YO! Sushi and panellist on *Dragons' Den*

'The principles of success apply equally whether you are an aspiring entrepreneur, chief executive of a large plc, or simply looking for inspiration for your own personal life. Here's where you start, by reading this book.'
Allan Leighton – Chairman, Royal Mail

'Entertaining, Inspiring, Insightful. I highly recommend it.'
Michelle Mone – MJM International

'In Millionaire MBA, *Richard decoded entrepreneurs and unpicked their millionaire mindset. With* Millionaire Upgrade, *he has put it all back together again through I BELIEVE and a compelling story. Very clever and a must read for any budding entrepreneur!'*
Rene Carayol – leadership guru

'In a world where entrepreneurs have taken on the cachet of celebrity, and are as often to be found portrayed in movies and in the gossip columns as they are seen with dirt under their fingernails, it is refreshing to find a book that describes the key difference between the entrepreneur and the rest – attitude. So often in life a cigarette paper's thickness separates success from failure, and Richard has written a book that perfectly captures this and suggests a way of thinking that can transform the tin of dog food into a thoroughbred racehorse. Read it, enjoy it, steal mercilessly from it, add your own ingredient X and bring to the boil. I wish you success.'
Tim Smit – Eden Project

'If you want a toolkit to help you become a successful entrepreneur – read this book. Then put it into practice.'
Duncan Bannatyne – Bannatyne Leisure and panellist on *Dragons' Den*

*'*Millionaire Upgrade *captures the essence of what it takes to be successful in anything you choose to do. The rules of success are timeless and simply explained so you can apply them in your own business or personal life.'*
B.J. Cunningham – founder of Death Cigarettes

'When you read Millionaire Upgrade, you will realize it is actually a book about leadership, leadership of self. I encourage all Naked Leaders to read this book.'
David Taylor – author of *The Naked Leader*

'The difference between success and failure in business is essentially down to entrepreneurial leadership. There is a mindset and persistence that sets successful entrepreneurs apart and it is clearly communicated in this book. Essential reading.'
Martin Allison – Business Banking, RBS

'Just reading the introduction I knew it was going to be good. Read, re-read and re-read again. It is all in here.'
Mike Southon – co-author of *The Beermat Entrepreneur*, *The Boardroom Entrepreneur* and *Sales on a Beermat*

'If you want success, then miss this at your peril. What Richard has done here, is make extremely accessible some very smart thinking and behaviours of highly successful people, which can be learned. This stuff really works.'
Michael Brook, Managing Director, Professional Excellence Training and Development

'Pioneers are always looking for succinct advice from experts. After submersing himself in the world of the entrepreneur, Richard gives us the answers in an intriguing role-play between two characters, with a genuine methodology that you can apply to your own business. You can read it on a plane journey, but the benefits will stay with you a long time after you've landed.'
Jim Woods – entrepreneur

'It takes a certain mindset to succeed in creating your own business. This book spells out how you need to think and act to succeed – whether you are an entrepreneur or a professional manager. It's a great read too.'
Matthew Barrett – Chairman, Barclays Bank

'Everything in business is a learning experience. I should know! I'd recommend all would-be entrepreneurs to read this book and be inspired to boldly set out on your own entrepreneurial journey. You won't regret it.'
Rachel Elnaugh – founder of Red Letter Days and panellist on *Dragons' Den*

For Jane, Amelia and My Parents

Richard Branson.

To me, Business isn't about
wearing suits or pleasing the stock
holders:
    It's about being true to your-
self, your ideas, and focusing
on the essentials

CONTENTS

ACKNOWLEDGEMENTS

I would like to sincerely thank everybody who has supported and helped me over the past few years as I've embarked upon a new journey as an entrepreneur.

In writing this book I would like to specifically thank my father for challenging me and always being there.

Anna Rushton and Nuala Mullen for their help and assistance in coaching me as a writer. John Moseley at Capstone Wiley and Simon Benham at Mayer Benham for help in making this book a reality.

I'd also like to thank Simon Woodroffe, Sir Tom Hunter and Sir Richard Branson for giving me the inspiration to write it – and all the other entrepreneurs and experts I have interviewed for *Millionaire MBA*; without them, there would be no book.

Thank you to Napoleon Hill, the father of this subject.

Thank you to George Zambartas who gave me the opportunity to start my speaking career and by virtue forced me to think differently about my material. Sincere thanks to Jason Murphy who planted the seed of an idea for a plot for *Millionaire Upgrade*, and to Philip Allen for giving me the idea of creating a mnemonic.

Special thanks and love to my wife Jane for putting up with me and believing in me. Special love to my daughter Amelia who asked me to tell everybody (but only those who needed to know).

INTRODUCTION

Like all good stories, the one you are about to read is inspired by actual events. Jason Murphy, one of the author's own family, was indeed upgraded on a flight in Australia where he was due to start a new business venture. Amazingly, he found himself sitting in seat 1B next to Sir Richard Branson who, during the trip, offered advice to this new entrepreneur. The characters in the book are inspired by real people.

Before writing this book I had interviewed 50 self-made millionaire entrepreneurs and many leading experts to create *Millionaire MBA* – an audio-based mentoring programme for business owners and aspiring entrepreneurs. The wisdom and insights in *Millionaire Upgrade* are drawn from this programme, and the fictional character of Michael represents the cumulative knowledge and experience of my interviews.

Michael's character was also specifically inspired by Tom Hunter, one of the entrepreneurs interviewed for the *Millionaire MBA* and one of Scotland's richest men. Tom started selling sports shoes from the back of his car after leaving school and eventually sold his business for over £280m. He has since gone on to increase that wealth to over £500m. In 2005, Tom was recognized by Her Majesty the Queen for his services to entrepreneurship and education and received a knighthood.

Sir Tom's favourite all-time entrepreneur was Andrew Carnegie (at one time the world's richest man) – a great philanthropist who left a legacy with his personal wealth, establishing 2,509 libraries throughout the English-speaking world. Sir Tom has continued in Andrew Carnegie's footsteps and is recognized as one of the UK's greatest philanthropists, having already pledged £100m of his personal wealth to enterprise and educational initiatives.

Andrew Carnegie also left another legacy. He recognized that the knowledge he gained in creating his own wealth was actually more important than the money itself and he made certain that his wisdom would not be lost after he died. For that reason, he commissioned Napoleon Hill, a young journalist, to spend his lifetime analyzing self-made millionaires and leaders of his time to uncover the common denominators which all successful people live by. Hill's book, *Think and Grow Rich,* is considered the accumulation of his life's work and is known and respected the world over.

It is *Think and Grow Rich* that inspired me to start investigating the common characteristics of modern self-made millionaire entrepreneurs, and it is no coincidence that the flight attendant who upgraded Tom in the book and gave him his 'magic ticket' was called Andrew, in homage to Andrew Carnegie.

The character of Tom is loosely based on me. This is partly because the book begins with Tom feeling just as I did (and thousands of other frustrated employees in the same position). The book follows his journey from this point through to him unveiling his business idea. Having created *Millionaire MBA* from scratch and taken the programme to market, I am also drawing from my own experience as an entrepreneur, having lived first-hand every message in this book.

It is a commonly held belief that successful entrepreneurs have something that sets them apart, a magic gene or special gift. What this book demonstrates, and what I hope you will take away with you, is that there is an accessible, common and consistent mindset that all of these individuals possess – the millionaire mindset. This mindset, as outlined in the book and the associated programme, can be learned, applied and shared – pass it on and enjoy the journey.

Richard Parkes Cordock
Author of *Millionaire Upgrade* and Creator of
***Millionaire MBA*™**
London 2005

FOREWORD

It is quite ironic, I believe, given the nature of this excellent book, that I write this foreword, as I listen to the in-flight airline radio. The man I am listening to is talking about the vision of HH Sheikh Mohammed bin Rashid Al Maktoum, Crown Prince of Dubai.

My family and I have just relocated to Dubai and we are very much looking forward to the new challenges that life will present.

I believe that in order to be successful in any undertaking in life, one must first have a vision. It is the starting point of all success and so I was highly delighted to be contacted by Richard Parkes Cordock, the author of *Millionaire Upgrade*, who had a great vision of how to bring this information to others, and who asked me to write this foreword.

I know from personal experience how influential the right book can be to really help you make changes. Approximately ten years ago, a book was recommended to me called *Think and Grow Rich*.

What was the point of reading a book that had been written in the 1930s, I thought to myself.

How wrong could I be! It was reading this book (which I know was also an inspiration to Richard) that helped me put into practice the principles for success and to realize a life-long goal by becoming World Snooker Champion.

After winning the World Snooker Championship in 2002, I was contacted by my former Latin tutor at Highbury Grove School in London. He asked me if I would be willing to deliver a motivational speech to the students there.

There were approximately 120 award winners in various subjects and I presented each student with a copy of the book that had originally inspired me in the hope that even if only one of them grasped the power and importance of the message and principles, then I would have helped to change that person's life forever.

Without any shadow of a doubt, reading that original book dramatically changed my life, and *Millionaire Upgrade* could do the same for you.

If you have already been successful in life or business, you will recognize a lot of the success principles in Richard's book. If you are on your journey to becoming successful, let me assure you that everything that you need to know is in here.

- What do you really, really want from life?
- Who do you want to be?
- What do you really want to achieve?
- Are you prepared to shape your life to ultimately achieve your goal?

If you are not prepared to pay the price in advance, the price you must pay ultimately, is not achieving your goal.

Perhaps the most important starting point is to really love what you are doing. Then, in the words of motivational guru Brian Tracy, 'Your work will become your play and your play will become your work.' You will happily work very hard to become the best that you can possibly be because you love what you are doing. It is your passion.

Passion is the thing that separates successful entrepreneurs and winners in sport, from others.

Perhaps one of my own personal strengths is my persistence. I believed wholeheartedly, and with absolute conviction, that I would be World Champion one day. It did take me 17 years and I made a lot of mistakes along the way, but I know that every single one of those mistakes was absolutely vital in my ultimate success. We learn and grow from making mistakes and that makes us much stronger.

Many people lose heart and give up when success doesn't happen when they want it to, but that is the crucial time. That is the point when focus, determination, persistence and belief, needs to be at its strongest because that is the period in which you will discover your 'alter ego'. That is the person inside of you that is so committed to achieving your goal that you will become like the strongest of laser beams, capable of blowing away any obstacle that stands in your way.

Always focus on your goal, not the obstacle, and your dreams and goals will come true.

When I needed things to come together for me and be at my strongest mentally, in order to become World Champion, I was.

In psychology, there is a term called 'colouring'. This is when desire, belief and love come together to form that irresistible, all-powerful, laser beam of concentration that enables you to achieve your goals.

For me, in the final frame of my 18–17 World Championship final victory over Stephen Hendry, the seven times World Champion and the most successful player in the history of the game, I focused all my attention, desire, belief and love for my wife and children, into a laser beam of concentration, to a level that I had never been to before. Perhaps it was through necessity but it was for me, out of love. I knew just how much it would mean to my wife, family and friends, for me to become World Champion and this is what I focused on.

That love, combined with an absolute belief in my ability to achieve my goal and a white-hot, all-consuming desire, took me to the top of my own personal mountain. And let me tell you that after all the hard work, disappointment, frustration, and at times disillusionment, the view from the top was absolutely magnificent!

It is something that I will treasure for the rest of my life.

The financial rewards were highly significant but far more importantly to me; I had achieved a life-long goal of something that could not be bought. I had paid the price in advance, believed in myself and in my abilities and got what I 'delivered'.

I believe that everything in life happens for a reason. I believe in cause and effect. Nothing happens by chance. Perhaps one of the most difficult things in life is to keep on keeping on, when success does not happen when we believe we deserve it.

You will only get out of life exactly what you put into it. It is a physical law from which there can be no deviation.

I very much like the line from one of the songs on Elton John's album, *Peachtree Road*, where he says 'we all get what we deliver'. I believe that he is correct.

My own personal formula for success is that:

preparation + opportunity + belief = RESULT.

And the result cannot be any greater or worse, than that which you deserve or deliver.

During my 17–16 World Championship semi-final win against Matthew Stevens, I visualized winning 17–16 (at 14–16 behind) so vividly, that I felt that I had already won!

A wave of certainty flowed through me and I held my nerve under the most extreme pressure to win an incredibly high-class match.

It is very easy however, to fall into the trap of becoming complacent or staying within your own personal comfort zone. I have been guilty of this over the past two seasons, despite knowing better. Knowing what to do is not enough. You must follow through and take massive action. You must grow and learn because we don't just stand still, we go backwards and then a greater amount of effort will be required to get your life back on track.

Millionaire Upgrade has helped me to re-focus and I would personally like to thank Richard, most sincerely, for putting me back on the right road.

Despite your knowledge, you will fail, if you fail to develop self-discipline.

Brian Tracy sums this up perfectly when he says 'do what you know you should do, when you should do it, whether you like it or not'. In short, self-discipline is the price of success.

Richard's book will take you on an incredible journey of self-discovery but ultimately your final destination will be entirely dependent upon you, your dedication, belief, desire and persistence.

In closing, I would like to say that I hope that we meet some day, possibly at an airport, so that we can share stories of how this wonderful book has made such a positive impact on our lives. Our final destinations may be different but with the help of *Millionaire Upgrade*, we will ALWAYS be on the same flight!

Kind regards,
Peter Ebdon, September 2005

Chapter One

How come, when you know how important it is, you still get it wrong? Tom knew he had set off too late for the airport. One more phone call, a last-minute panic to find his project notes, and a final cup of coffee were the perfect procrastinator's menu for what he now had on his plate. Frustrated and anxious, he was sitting on the express shuttle to the terminal, watching the seconds tick away and cursing himself, yet again, for not leaving the house earlier. Check-in was due to close an hour before departure and things weren't looking good. He bounced nervously on the balls of his feet, his lean frame pressed against the tightly closed doors, almost willing the train to go faster. Finally! As they pulled in, Tom was the first out and running up the escalator and straight into the check-in area.

While Tom was burning up every last ounce of energy sprinting to the desk, a man in his 50s, dressed in an expensive-looking dark linen suit with a crisp open neck shirt, was quietly talking on his phone and making notes with an elegant silver fountain pen on that day's copy of the business pages. He politely declined a cup of coffee, with a smile and a wave of the hand, and stayed totally focused on his conversation.

As Tom arrived at the check-in desk his heart sank as he realized there was no one else queuing. Was he too late? He smiled hopefully at the blonde woman at check-in while handing over his passport and ticket and she gave them a quick glance.

'I can check you in here, but you're too late for me to allocate you a seat. If you go straight to gate number thirteen you'll be on standby, and they'll give you more information. Quick as you can please as the flight is closing.'

Tom momentarily worried about that number thirteen as yet another bad sign on a less than perfect day so far, but grabbed his briefcase and set off at a run to the far end of the terminal for the departure gate. Hot and sweaty, but not too out of breath, he arrived to see a line of passengers already getting on the plane. Approaching the man at the desk he explained the situation, expecting to board immediately. The attendant's nametag read 'Andrew' and he had a soft Scottish burr as he explained to Tom that he would have to wait until the last passenger had boarded before they could seat him. So he waited, with an increasing feeling of dread that actually there would turn out to be no seat at all. Andrew kept glancing over and smiling reassuringly and turned his attention to the man who had just strolled unhurriedly up to the gate. It was the man Tom had observed earlier at check-in. He really looked like a man who was used to the best things in life. Andrew greeted him respectfully, but with familiarity, and appeared to be asking him some questions. The man glanced round and looked at Tom with a warm smile, then turned back and nodded. As he went through to the plane, Andrew beckoned Tom over to hear the words he had most feared.

'I'm sorry sir, but the flight is full and all the tickets in economy are assigned.'

I knew it, thought Tom. This is not my day. As his face mirrored his disappointment and frustration, Andrew quickly spoke again.

'Not to worry sir, you're a frequent flyer with us, we can upgrade you as there's a seat in business class. The gentleman who has just gone through normally books two seats and he's agreed to let you have one. That means we can upgrade you to seat 1B, the second best seat on the plane, and really a much better way to travel! Have a good flight.' Smiling, he handed over the boarding card and removed the rope barrier for Tom to go through.

Hardly able to believe his luck, Tom went on board where he was ushered quickly to his seat and he strapped himself in for imminent take-off. He was rushed and agitated, but these days it wasn't a new feeling, and he nodded gratefully to the man who was now his travelling companion. He couldn't help noticing that he looked calm and relaxed, so Tom took a steadying breath as he turned to him.

'I really appreciate you doing this for me. It would have been disastrous if I'd missed the flight. Thanks very much.'

He held his hand out and they exchanged a quick, firm, handshake. His companion smiled at him in a friendly fashion and replied.

'No problem. Perhaps we should introduce ourselves as we are going to be together quite some time? My name is Michael, Michael Redford, and it's good to have some company. He looked enquiringly at Tom as two stewardesses passed them checking that the overhead lockers were closed and that everyone was wearing their seat belts.

'I'm Tom, Tom McMillan. Lucky for me there was a spare seat because, to be honest, I only got bumped up because I was too late to get into the regular seat I had booked. So thank you again'.

Michael was settling himself comfortably. 'Hey, like I said it's no problem. I always have two seats booked in case my assistant travels with me, or just to have a bit more breathing space.' He looked at Tom enquiringly. 'Did you have a problem with transport? I hear there was a big traffic hold-up on the main road out of the city.'

'No, it wasn't the traffic. I just kept getting delayed when I was trying to leave. Too much to do and I always seem to be in a rush these days!'

Michael nodded sympathetically. 'In my younger days I was always rushing too, so I remember what it's like, and as I said, I'm happy to help out.' Michael settled himself back and adjusted his seat belt as Tom ran his hands over the leather upholstery and smiled in relief and delight at this unexpected comfort. The stewardesses were now demonstrating the safety procedures, and as Tom looked around, his neighbour unhurriedly uncapped his pen and took a leather-bound notebook out of his pocket. Tom slipped a book out of his pocket and reflected that at least he had the chance to read in comparative quiet. It was a business success book he had picked up earlier, one of the many he had looked at over the last few months. Some had been useful, but none had managed to help him see what to do about his current situation. He knew he wanted more from his life; he knew he wanted to make a real success of it. Before starting to read he studied the back cover closely. Could it be, he thought, that this might be the book to give him clues as to how to get out of the potentially disastrous situation he was in? It had been brewing for the last three months and was now definitely coming to the boil. He turned the book over, preparing to read, and Michael glanced over in an interested fashion as he caught sight of the title *Think and Grow Rich*.

'That's an interesting choice of book. You don't see many young men reading that these days. Napoleon Hill can teach you a lot.' He smiled at Tom. 'It will give you some of the tools to make a real success of your life. I learned a lot from reading that book at the very beginning of my career, and I see you want to know 'the secret' too.'

Tom was intrigued. He had not heard of this particular book before he bought it and he was surprised Michael had heard of the author. No one at his software company had ever mentioned reading about business success; in fact, reading anything other than project manuals was seen as weird. 'I picked it up yesterday, but I thought it was new.'

His companion smiled. 'Well actually it's been around a very long time. Written in the 1930s *I believe*, but it certainly helped me learn the principles that made all the difference to how my life developed. In fact *I believe* it gave me some of the guiding principles that helped in my own business success. I hope it does the same for you.'

The plane was now taxiing down the runway, and as Tom glanced out of the window he glimpsed the open page where Michael had begun making notes. It looked like calculations that had quite a lot of noughts on the end and Tom wondered just how successful Michael was. That remark about 'the secret' was certainly interesting but would he be willing to actually tell Tom what it was? Really, Tom thought, all I need are a few clues on how to move forward. As he hesitated, the 'unfasten seat belt' lights went on, and as he unbuckled he wondered how to approach the subject. Michael helped him out by leaning forward and asking:

'So, what kind of business are you in, Tom?'

This was a question Tom had recently been asking himself fairly frequently, and he had even started to wonder if in fact he really was in the right business. He debated just how much to tell Michael and was on the point of giving a short, snappy answer when he suddenly thought 'what have I got to lose, I might as well get another perspective on it. This guy is obviously successful, so he might be able to give me some good advice.'

'I'm an IT project manager. Well, I am at the moment. But this trip may be my last for the company as there is a lot of change going on right now and there's some talk of downsizing and redundancy. It may not affect me directly, but if I'd missed this flight it wouldn't have looked good for me. I'm not looking forward to the job I've been given to do on this trip, but it wouldn't be any easier if I had missed the flight and delayed it. I'd rather just get it over with.'

'Business is often about doing things you would rather not do,' said Michael. '*I believe* that if I'm not working on something I'm passionate about, or believe in, then it can seem like an uphill struggle. What is the unpleasant task, if you don't mind my asking?'

Tom realized that he was only too happy to talk about it, particularly to a stranger who wasn't involved. 'No, I don't mind. In fact it's good to be able to talk about it. I'm going out to close down our regional office and get everything transferred back to base. It's been running down for a while now, but it's not the work so much as the people. Some of them may not get other jobs, and things aren't looking good for the company at home either. At the moment it feels like I'm chasing my tail the whole time.'

'Sounds frustrating,' remarked Michael sympathetically and encouraging him to go on.

Tom nodded in agreement. 'That's my constant state these days. The problem is I work in software development and it changes so fast it's hard to keep up. It's like being on a treadmill; just when you think you're getting somewhere another new product comes in and you have to start all over again. I'm really struggling to stay on top of it, and to be honest, things are just not going that well. The rumours of redundancy or redeployment within the company make it all the more uncertain and hard to keep focused on what you are doing. It's difficult to feel you're making a success of something when you're mostly just running to keep up. I've been reading a lot of business success books recently, but just how to change things seems to be eluding me.' He sighed quietly. 'I wish I knew what to do about it.'

Suddenly embarrassed by his confidence to a stranger, Tom hurriedly tried to change the subject, but Michael didn't react the way he would have expected. He just shrugged and said: 'You know that's often how it is in life. Success and failure are two sides of the same coin and I *believe* it can be flipped over whenever you choose.'

Tom wondered if Michael had actually heard what he had said. The possibility of being made redundant, or his job downgraded, certainly didn't give him the feeling that he had control over his current situation. Deciding whether he was going to be a success or a failure, well, that certainly wasn't how it appeared to him. It was the company who had all the options, from what he could see, so he decided to challenge Michael about it.

'Surely success is a matter of luck to some degree; you can't just turn it around. It isn't always within your control, circumstances can prevent you,' he said, facing Michael with a questioning look on his face.

'On the contrary Tom, *I believe* that success is based on eight sound principles or insights if you like, that once learned and applied can do just that. *I believe* it is always in your control; whether you choose to exercise it of course is up to you.' Michael smiled at Tom's obvious scepticism. 'You don't believe me do you? Well, tell me a bit more about your problem at work and I will see if I can help.'

Tom felt suddenly optimistic, but quickly pushed it aside. He had spent too many months worrying about his situation to believe that there could be an easy answer just like that. However, this was a great opportunity, and he must have been put in this seat for a reason, so why not take advantage of it? He indicated to the pen and notebook and said 'It looks as if you are planning on doing some work, so I don't want to interrupt you, but yeah, I'd really like to get another opinion.'

Michael nodded and put the notebook and pen down. 'OK. What's the real problem?'

Tom was taken aback: 'The real problem?'

'Well', Michael said, 'in my experience the actual thing you think is the problem is usually just a sign of something deeper that is wrong, so I like to get to that first. It saves time!'

Tom laughed at that, and thought for a moment. 'Well, I have wondered if it's my job. I'm a project manager in an IT company, as I said, but I just don't really like going in anymore. I dread the constant repetition of the stuff I do, and each day is the same: chasing deadlines and never having a moment to breathe. But if it's not my job ...' His voice tailed off and he tried to think about what Michael had said. 'The real problem, I think, is that I feel stuck, and bored. I'm frustrated and although I want something better, different, I don't know where to start.' He gestured towards the book in his lap. 'I told you I've been reading books like this for a while now and although I know there's a better future out there, I just don't know how to get there.'

Michael nodded in agreement. 'Well, the good news is that you're absolutely right. There is a better future and there are clues to help you find it. Let's see if I can help you identify what those clues are. Take myself for example, what do you see when you look at me?'

Tom wasn't sure what reply Michael was hoping for, but he looked at him and debated for a moment or two about the impression Michael had made on him. 'Well, I see a man who is obviously very successful in business, used to the good life and all its benefits, like travelling in the best seat in the plane! Probably privately educated, then university, probably a serious business background and someone who likes beautiful things.' He indicated the pen. 'I don't know much about it, but that looks like a valuable antique to me.'

'You're right about the pen!' said Michael as he ran his finger over the silver scrollwork on the body. 'I bought that when I made my first million and it combines form and function with beauty – and that's important to me. But as for the rest, if I was to give myself a label, I'm an entrepreneur and I certainly wasn't born with a silver spoon in my mouth! In fact, my family sold things from a stall at an open air market, and

I left school at 16 with no qualifications at all. You see Tom, *I believe* it's a person's experience and what they do with it that matters, not where they come from or how educated they are.' Michael saw Tom was looking quite surprised. 'It's not what you expected is it?'

Tom shook his head, and then smiled. 'You're right, I didn't think you were an entrepreneur, maybe a CEO of a major corporation or something similar, but not that. You know I've often thought about running my own business, but I lose heart because it always seems like the people doing it possess something above and beyond the rest of us. They had to have special qualities, things I don't think I have.'

Michael looked at him. 'You're right, they do have special qualities, but they're the same ones that everyone else has. You already have all of them, it's whether you choose to use them and how you do it that makes the difference between having an entrepreneur or an employee mindset.' Tom noticed he was looking at him seriously as if weighing him up. 'Tom, let me ask you a question. Which mindset do you think you have – that of a millionaire, or an employee?'

Tom was startled and wondered how on earth to reply. 'I'm not really familiar with the concept. Can you expand on that a bit?'

'Sure' Michael said. 'OK, *I believe* we are all born potential millionaires. It's our genetic destiny to achieve because we are a race of 'positive creators'. You know, everything we see has been created in our minds first, and if you think about it, to be an entrepreneur means that you have to create something out of nothing. Everyone has the ability, but the problem is that most people are only using a tiny fraction of their potential.

Most people are stuck in the mindset they've inherited from their parents and that's the first thing that has to change. They usually teach us to get a good education and qualifications, so we can get a good job where we'll be promoted and build a solid pension. Certainly that's safe, but very few people I know have ever achieved financial freedom that way.'

'But hang on a minute', said Tom. 'Are you saying those are bad things?'

'Not good or bad, but what I just described is the employee mindset where you work for someone else and they dictate how, when and where you work. How many people in regular jobs are there who get to be a millionaire just from their salary?'

'Well, apart from a handful of high-flying financial city types, not many.'

Michael went on: 'The millionaire mindset is a 180 degree shift from the employee mindset so that you are following your passion, not your pension. You get so obsessed with your business idea that you just can't stop thinking about it, you are so excited by it. Do you understand the difference?'

Whilst Tom understood it, he was still not sure how it could be applied to him. 'How do I switch from one to the other?'

'Well Tom, you work in IT so this should be really simple for you. I said you need to change your mindset and the mind is just a computer. So all you need to do is reprogramme it with some new software!'

Grateful to Michael for using an analogy he could relate to, Tom started to relax. 'Oh, I can do that alright.' He was now alert and interested and stood up to get his briefcase out of the overhead locker. Michael glanced questioningly up at him and looking down over his shoulder Tom explained:

'I have the feeling that the things you're saying could be really important to me. If you don't mind I'd like to write them down, so I don't forget them.'

Smiling, Michael tore out the page from his notebook with his calculations on and handed the notebook over to Tom.

'Here, use mine. I always carry a notebook because, as you just found out, you never know when you need to write down something that has inspired or interested you, or a great idea strikes you.'

Tom held the slim notebook in his hand and then pulled a pen from his jacket pocket and started to write down the key things that Michel had told him so far.

'OK, I understand the difference between millionaire and employee mindset, but there must be more to it than that?'

Nodding, Michael watched Tom's notes appearing on the page.

'Of course, and you also need to know much more about the eight clear principles or elements. Anyone can apply them, but most people don't do it for a variety of reasons, or they only apply a couple.' He waited until Tom had written down '8 principles' and then he went on. 'Do you remember as a child ever seeing at the circus someone spinning plates on sticks, starting with one or two and ending up with six or eight all going at the same time?'

He didn't immediately see the relevance of a circus act in their conversation, but Tom was realizing that Michael never said anything without a good reason so he nodded in agreement.

'You saw those plates in the air and they were all spinning at once. The juggler had to pay attention to every single plate, not just the ones nearest him. If he let his focus slip, or didn't pay them equal attention, then what happened?'

'They fell crashing round his ears!' Tom jotted down another note, and then heard the slight rattling sound of a drinks trolley approaching them. One of the stewardesses he had seen earlier approached them and offered Tom a glass of champagne. Michael was clearly well known to her and she handed him a beer without being asked. 'Never been much of a champagne man', smiled Michael. He then greeted the stewardess with easy familiarity, asked how she was doing and enquired about how her husband was coping with early retirement. Tom realized that Michael was indeed a very frequent traveller and well known to the airline staff.

The stewardess smiled back, delighted at him remembering their last conversation, and said everything was fine. Her husband was finally doing all the things he had really wanted to do, and that she was looking forward to early retirement too so she could join him. This was obviously a familiar joke between them, and Michael teased her as she prepared to move down the cabin.

'Olivia, you know you can't retire until I do, and that's not for quite a few years yet!'

Tom raised his glass to his nose and sniffed appreciatively at the flowery bouquet. He made a toast to Michael as he drank.

'Well, here's to the champagne lifestyle. You don't get this in economy! If this is what being a successful entrepreneur is like, then I'm all in favour of it!'

Michael laughed, and said 'So that's why you are reading *Think and Grow Rich*! I admit the title might make you think it's all about money, but if you think fine wines and luxury are what primarily motivates entrepreneurs then you're wrong. Of course, only a fool would say the money isn't important, but it's not as important as why you want to run your own business, and the passion that drives you to do it.'

Tom objected, 'Come on, surely the money is why everyone does it?'

Michael shook his head. 'No, it's why people *think* they want to do it, but without all the other principles coming into play you will never be successful over the long term if all you are focusing on is the money. Remember the juggler – it's never about just one plate!'

Tom really was intrigued now. 'The money would certainly help me. I'm in danger of losing my job, and Julie, my fiancée, and I are planning on marrying next year.'

Michael nodded. 'Of course it would help, but what I'm really saying is that if you find out what drives you, then you have a chance to be successful beyond what you can imagine.' He thought for a moment, and then continued. 'Let me ask you a question. Why do you work in IT rather than in any other profession?'

'I guess I just drifted into it', replied Tom. 'I would never say I was passionate about it, but I was generally interested and, more importantly, I needed some income after university. It had a great salary, and when I was offered the job I had huge student debts and credit card bills. So, I suppose you could say that in many ways I did it for the money!'

'OK, I will give you that! And is it still a good salary?' asked Michael.

'Yes, it is', Tom agreed.

'Then if it was just about the money for you, why are you not satisfied now?' remarked Michael. '*I believe* that it's because deep down, success as an entrepreneur is never about the money. It is about freedom, choice, proving yourself, doing things your own way, creating what you need to create.'

Tom was really struck by the sincerity and depth of passion in Michael's voice. This was something that he absolutely believed in and he started jotting down the key words as Michael continued.

'When an entrepreneur starts a business, they usually need to do it because the pain they feel of not doing it is so great, or the pain of carrying on for the rest of their lives as an employee is so great – that they have no real alternative. Of course, it is also true that money plays a part in it – when you have no money and the prospect of having some is great, then the need for money is a good driver – but I meet very few successful entrepreneurs who just do it for the money.' Tom was looking thoughtful, so Michael pressed on. 'You on the other hand, are working just to pay the bills. *I believe* that is why you're unhappy at work and looking for answers in books like *Think and Grow Rich.*'

Tom wasn't sure why, but he really didn't like hearing himself described as someone who was working just to pay the bills. That sounded like everyone else he knew, and made him seem too predictable, accepting his life just as it was. He didn't think of himself as predictable, but when Michael talked he could see his life stretching out before him, dull, flat and inevitable. He was suddenly reminded of his father and how he had quietly soldiered on for years in a job he neither liked nor disliked. If he had had dreams Tom did not know what they were, and he suddenly felt trapped and irritated at himself for feeling like that. Michael saw his discomfort and waited for Tom to get his thoughts together.

Tom put his champagne glass down and thought about what he wanted to ask Michael. Lots of questions were running through his head, and he knew that his being in this seat on this plane was the most incredibly lucky break and that he had to seize it. He knew this was a once in a lifetime opportunity and thanked his lucky stars that he had got this seat. In fact he felt like he was going through his own personal master class with someone who was obviously a very successful self-made millionaire. However, his old habit of self-doubt made him cautious. Although he wasn't sure Michael really would let him in on all his secrets, if he wasn't going to go for it now, he might never get another chance.

'OK, if it isn't the money, then what is it? I warn you I have lots of other questions too!'

Satisfied, Michael leaned back and thought for a moment. 'I'm delighted you have lots of questions, because *I believe* that it is from the mind that it all starts.' He looked over at Tom. 'Tell me, what are you really passionate about?'

Tom looked surprised. He had his pen poised to make notes on how to be successful; he wasn't prepared for a question about something so vague. 'I guess. Well … I don't know really', he said slowly as he realized that actually he had never allowed himself to think about that.

'Not your job then?' asked Michael with a twinkle in his eye.

'Not at all' replied Tom. 'To be honest, when I think about my job I see this treadmill with endless deadlines stretching ahead of me, and whenever you reach them you have to start all over again doing the same thing. I know what the company wants is a very fast turnaround that will keep the customers happy with the minimum of input, but that doesn't satisfy me. The clients are unhappy because they aren't getting my undivided attention and I don't master the new software completely before the next one is launched and I have to start all over again with the new one. No, I certainly don't feel passionate about my work. Frustrated and fed up is more like it!'

Michael looked at him speculatively. 'Do you know why I got started in business?' As Tom looked ready to respond he continued on. 'It was because as a young boy I was obsessed with running. That was my passion. I was a sprinter but in those days good training shoes were few and far between. My uncle had a market stall selling boots and slippers and he got a few pairs of trainers in for me to try. They were OK, but I always wanted something better, faster, lighter, so I started trying to find suppliers so my uncle could stock them on the stall, but he wasn't really interested. So, I started selling them myself, first to my school friends and then I got my own market stall. From my passion for running I ended up owning first one sports shop, and then a chain, which I sold for over a hundred million. In fact, you could say my business came out of the problem I had in not being able to satisfy my passion for great running shoes.'

Tom had been listening fascinated. This successful looking clean-cut man certainly didn't look as if he had ever seen a market stall, let alone run one! He thought for a moment, then said 'I wish I could say I had a passion like that. I have often thought I would like to run a business but really I have no idea where to start. Over the last year I have read lots of books, listened to motivational business programmes and really made a study of success. I have loved doing that, but I still have no idea where my passion would lie.'

Michael was struck by the intensity in Tom's voice. He obviously was sincere and so much wanted to have some answers to his problems that Michael knew he had to try and help him. 'Think back a few years. Were there no interests or hobbies that you were completely absorbed by, almost addicted to?'

Tom closed his eyes for a few seconds as if looking at an internal screen where he was reviewing his life. Slowly he nodded, and had a reminiscent smile on his face. 'Yes, actually you're right. I was a very good junior tennis player, and I kept that up until I went to university. Unfortunately once I started all that academic work, to say nothing of the social life, I just let it drop because there didn't seem enough time. So that was something that I was passionate about once, I loved playing tennis. I felt totally alive; I never even minded the training!'

Michael had been watching Tom's face and seen the light in it, and how his voice had changed to sounding full of energy and conviction. He thought he would try and go a bit deeper. 'What do you think made you a good tennis player then, Tom?'

'Oh, I suppose I was passionate about it, to use your word. When I was playing I thought about nothing else and when I stepped on that court I believed that I was unbeatable. I was obsessed, I wanted to win so badly and everything just seemed to fall into place when I was playing.'

Michael grinned at him. 'You have just described some of the key characteristics of successful entrepreneurs: passion, desire and self-belief. No business can succeed unless you are really passionately obsessed and have a burning desire to succeed. You must love the challenge, and you can only do that when you are operating from your passion. It's where you connect your heart and your mind together. Like when you are in love. Remember when you first met your fiancée? Julie wasn't it? You had to move right out of your comfort zone to ask her out, and you did it. We do amazing things for love: take risks, conquer our fears and our limiting beliefs – all because of love. It can truly create magic in our lives and that's why it's the first step, to find that passion for an idea, a service or a business. Did you win any trophies for your tennis?'

Tom wondered if Michael was signalling that he wanted to turn the conversation into more general areas, but here at least was something he could boast about! 'Quite a few. I used to take them home and my parents would put them on a shelf and proudly point them out to visitors.'

'Were they valuable trophies?' Michael asked.

Startled, Tom laughed. 'Not at all, they were not expensive silver or anything like that. Probably worth very little, but I never even thought about it.'

'So', Michael persisted. 'If they weren't worth much, you weren't playing for material gains were you? So what were you playing for?'

Tom thought about it. 'For the pleasure of winning and competing. Every match was a challenge that I had to over-come. I never thought about anything else.'

'Exactly!' said Michael. Still think being successful is all about money?'

Tom held his hands up in front of him in mock surrender. 'OK, it's true that the winning wasn't about money, but I'm still not convinced it isn't the major factor for most people. I know that making a million would have a major impact on my life and circumstances right now!'

Michael could see that Tom was resistant to the idea that passion was more important than money and he realized he had to get Tom to think a bit more deeply.

'OK, so you are not sure it's the money. Well, I know a lot of very successful entrepreneurs, all millionaires and some of them even billionaires. All of them have more than enough money to retire and live in luxury for the rest of their lives. And yet, they don't do it. They aren't sitting on a beach contemplating the ocean; they are out there starting new businesses. So if it isn't the money that is driving them, what do you think it is?'

'How about greed', Tom flashed back, then laughed as he watched Michael's eyebrow go up, but he continued on. 'Well, if they are going on making millions then there must be a good reason for it and greed is a reason for some people. Most of us would just think about going off around the world, living on a golf course and playing 18 holes every day, so when I read stories in the business news about millionaires who don't retire I do wonder why. Are you telling me that it is just passion that keeps them going?'

'Yes I am, and I'm also telling you that to be successful you have to stop thinking like 'most of us' to use your phrase', said Michael. 'We just talked about love a few minutes ago. Successful entrepreneurs are so in love with their business that they can't think of anything more interesting and vital to be doing than working on that business. Even when they are sitting on that beach and looking at the ocean, they are still thinking about their business because when you're passionate and motivated to do something then you're literally 'white hot' with desire to make something happen.' Michael grinned, 'Whether that's getting the girl of your dreams or starting your own company, the passion is the same.'

Tom was really enjoying himself now. This conversation was more fun than he had experienced in a while and he had the feeling it was really taking him somewhere he wanted to go. 'Right Michael, I surrender! It's about passion, but now I don't play tennis any more, so where does that leave me?'

Michael smiled. 'You just have to find the thing that can raise your energy and get you fired up in exactly the same way. It can be an idea, a product, a service or anything that makes you feel alive and confident that nothing else matters as much as that does. Find that, and *I believe* you will start thinking like a successful entrepreneur – maybe even like a self-made millionaire.'

Tom looked up from writing in his notebook as something Michael said struck him. 'I just realized that you say "I believe" quite a lot. Is that deliberate?'

'Yes' said Michael. 'I do, because as I told you self-belief is critical to success. Saying *I believe* is a little device of mine to remind me of what I need to do to stay successful.

Tom looked sceptical. 'But just saying "I believe" won't bring that kind of success.'

Michael laughed heartily as he shook his head. 'No of course not: just saying something doesn't change anything. Acting on it is what makes the difference. For me, *I believe* represents the principles of success that I have seen over and over again. Each letter of *I believe* gives me clues to the qualities I'm looking for in myself, and in any project I'm going to take on. We have already discussed the 'I' and the 'B' for instance.'

Tom looked puzzled. 'We have?'

Michael nodded. 'Certainly we have. You for instance probably didn't register the 'I' because you are still thinking like an employee. The 'I' stands for **I believe in myself**. It's all about self-belief and it has to be total. You must have an almost unnerving belief in your ability to reach your goals.'

Tom wasn't sure about that. 'Sounds like arrogance to me', he said.

'No, it's very different believe me', said Michael. 'You cannot pursue your goals if you don't believe in them one hundred per cent. It's not thinking that *you* are great, but that your *idea* is unbeatable and that you'll do anything to make your customers believe in your product or service as much as you do. That's where the 'B' of believe comes in. This stands for **Be passionate and want it**. You have to be totally in love with your idea and have a burning desire to make it happen.

'Just remember when you are passionate about something you will do it, whatever happens. It's your overwhelming desire that will give you the determination, drive and ultimately the commitment that you need to realize your business idea. It is all about belief – absolutely, with no doubts, believe in what you are doing, be totally passionate about your business idea, and be sure that it is something you would do even if you weren't getting paid for it. Not getting any trophies, for instance!'

Tom laughed and looked up eagerly. 'Right if that's 'I' and 'B', what's next?'

'Obviously it's the rest of the letters from *I believe*! But, first have a think over what I have just said, do some soul-searching to find what it is that you're passionate about and what you believe in and we'll get onto the rest later.' Michael stood up, stretched and strolled his way up the aisle. Although Tom was hoping for the secret of his success there and then, he smiled to himself as he realized that Michael wanted him to do some of the work too, and carried on writing in his notebook.

TOM'S NOTES

① BELIEVE — I BELIEVE IN MYSELF

- There is a millionaire mindset and an employee mindset — it is your choice which one you have.
- There are eight principles of success — you need to make sure you practise all of them all of the time.
- You must develop unnerving belief in yourself as an entrepreneur (this is not arrogance, but self-belief).
- You can develop self-belief and confidence by stepping outside of your comfort zone.
- Self-doubt is the death of an entrepreneur.

I (B)ELIEVE –
BE PASSIONATE AND WANT IT

- Passion and love for your idea is the starting point as an entrepreneur.
- You must connect your heart and your head together around your winning business idea.
- You must have a motive for becoming a successful entrepreneur. Money is not a strong enough motivator. Pursuit of passion or avoidance of pain is!
- If you do something that you are motivated for, passionate about and believe in, then untold magic will happen.

Chapter Two

As Tom sat back and thought about what Michael had said, he was aware of the drinks trolley coming back down the aisle towards him. Olivia drew level to his seat, smiled at him. 'Have you finished with your glass sir?' Tom nodded, handed it over, and as she was about to turn away his curiosity got the better of him. He had been thinking about her remarks about her husband and his early retirement and for some reason what she said had stuck in his mind.

'Do you mind my asking, but what kind of things is your husband doing now that he is retired?' he asked.

She looked a little surprised at his question, but smiled and nodded as she stowed his glass away safely on the trolley.

'Well, he has always drawn and painted ever since I met him and now he can devote all his time to it. Over the years he has had a few local exhibitions that he got a really good response to and he sold some paintings, which was wonderful!'

'Then, I just wondered why he has waited until he's retired to do it full-time?' queried Tom, hoping she wouldn't think he was being rude.

Olivia hesitated. 'I'm not sure why, but probably security had a lot to do with it. The time never seemed to be right, but I'm sure if he had done, he could have made a success of it.'

'Thanks' said Tom 'I appreciate you telling me. I really wish him well now he's finally doing what he always wanted.'

She looked a little startled, then slowly nodded as if in agreement.

'I guess he is, and thanks for your good wishes.' She moved away down the aisle, leaving Tom reflecting on what she had just said. He just couldn't bear the thought of waiting until he retired to do something that really inspired him, and that he really wanted to do. He was deep in thought and jumped when Michael tapped him lightly on the shoulder as he stood beside him in the aisle.

'You really were miles away weren't you? Have I given you food for thought?' Michael asked him as he settled back down in his own seat.

'Yes you have, but I was thinking more of something I just asked the stewardess.'

'Olivia? What did you want to know?' Michael looked at him curiously.

Tom unconsciously raised his hands as he turned to reply, as if he was trying to shape his answer before he spoke. 'Well, I asked about her husband's retirement and it made me realize I don't want to wait that long to do something I really want to do.'

'Was it just that?' Michael asked him and Tom hesitated before saying:

'No. It was more what she said about why he had waited, about the time being right, and not wanting to take the leap and do the very thing he was passionate about.'

Michael grinned and leaned over and tapped the notebook that was still on Tom's lap. 'I think you're ready for the next part of I believe! Still interested?'

As if a switch had been turned on inside him, Tom realized that there was nothing he wanted more than to discover the rest of the secret to I believe. He opened the notebook and turned to Michael.

'OK'. Michael leaned back in his chair and held up his left hand with the fingers splayed out. With his right hand he touched the fingers as he counted. 'First we had the letter "I", which stands for "I believe", then the "B" for "Be passionate and want it". 'Now', he lightly touched his middle finger 'we have the "E", and you have just described it to me perfectly.'

'Have I?' Tom asked. 'I wasn't aware of it!'

'No' agreed Michael 'but that's just because you didn't recognize what it was. The "E" is to **Extend your comfort zone**, and that's probably the reason Olivia's husband never quit his job to become a full-time artist. He was afraid to get out of where he felt safe.'

'But surely' Tom countered, 'most of us operate in our comfort zone? Is that so wrong?'

'No, not necessarily' agreed Michael, 'that is if you want to be "most of us", but I thought you wanted something better? If you never face your fears about the future and conquer them, then you will never be successful. We all need to be stretched as human beings in order to grow, but if you don't allow yourself to be challenged then you actually shrink. Your self-confidence diminishes and you are simply not being true to yourself. You need to expand your comfort zone by doing something every day that makes you uncomfortable. That's the way you will move forward.'

Tom felt a bit daunted by this, but looking into Michael's calm face he realized that here was someone who, after all, had obviously done that and was sitting here in the best seat in the plane, so he must know what he was talking about. Guardedly, he asked him, 'You mean I must take risks more often, right?'

'No' replied Michael. 'It isn't necessarily about taking more risks, but we'll definitely be talking about risk later on.'

Pausing momentarily, he looked Tom in the eyes so that he really understood the impact of what he was telling him. 'What I'm saying is that to be successful, you must do more things that make you feel uncomfortable, up to a level of discomfort that shows you that you are indeed moving forward. Let's try a little experiment. Are you up for it?'

'OK. I'm game. What do I have to do?' Tom sat forward in his seat ready for whatever task Michael might set him.

'Nothing too taxing – don't worry' he reassured him. 'Now just cross your arms in front of your chest.'

Tom was a bit bemused, but played along with it. Michael solemnly looked at him, but there was definitely a twinkle in his eye.

'Now just notice which arm is on top. Most of us have a dominant side and you will always cross your arms the same way.'

Tom looked down and realized he had automatically crossed his arms so his left arm was on top.

'Now reverse that so the other arm is on top.' Michael watched in amusement as Tom tried to change over and still ended up with the same arm on top! He tried again, and when he had done it Michael nodded. 'Now just sit that way for a few minutes. How does it feel?'

'Weird! It is just not natural. I don't feel comfortable.'

'No, it isn't natural and that's exactly the point.' Michael agreed. 'It's a small thing, but it has moved you out of your comfort zone. You could also try brushing your teeth with the opposite hand for a few days, but that's not so easy at 30,000 feet!'

Tom looked uncomfortable, but Michael wasn't letting him off the hook.

'Stay like that a bit longer to see if the feeling changes. Let me give you another example. Do you remember when you first met your future fiancée and were you nervous about asking her out?'

Here we go again, thought Tom, he's going off on another of those sidetracks he seems to like so much! But he nodded in agreement as Michael continued.

'Well, you were afraid, but you wanted to get to know her so you plucked up your courage and asked her out. Now if you'd wanted to play it safe you could have waited and found out more about her, see if you knew anyone who knew her and try and find out if she was interested in you. By that time she could have met someone else and you would have been too late. But you found the courage to ask her out. You pushed yourself outside your comfort zone and you got the reward. She's now your fiancée. You tell me, was it worth feeling uncomfortable for?'

'Absolutely', said Tom, unconsciously relaxing back into his seat without noticing that his arms felt a bit more comfortable.

'Well then, you understand one of the basic principles of becoming a successful entrepreneur.' Once again Michael ticked off the points on his fingers. 'You have to start spending a lot of time feeling uncomfortable, face your fears and take some action. You risked looking like a fool if she had turned you down, but you were willing to put yourself out there. Let's face it, rejection and failure is part and parcel of life, but the successful entrepreneur is willing to accept that as the norm, deal with it, and carry on. You showed you could do that for love, so why not for business?'

'Hang on a minute!' Tom leaned forward, his eyes were laughing and his whole face showed an energy Michael hadn't seen in him before. 'Are you telling me that love and business are the same?'

'No. I'm telling you that to be successful in business you have to love what you do. Remember that was the "B" – Be passionate and want it, now you are looking at what you have to do for the next stage, and that is the realization that success lies on the other side of comfort. Sure you can just stay where you are for the rest of your life, you've already told me you have a good salary, you have security, but you're not happy. *I believe* that in order to be true to ourselves we have to take total responsibility and have the courage to make the necessary sacrifices to gain the rewards that we want. Tom, most people – to use your terminology – use only five to ten per cent of their potential. Can you honestly tell me that you are making the most of your talents and abilities right now?'

While he had been listening, Tom hadn't noticed that he had been holding his breath. Now, he let it out slowly, realizing the tension that had been slowly developing in him. He felt Michael was challenging him to step up to the plate and he knew that somewhere along the line he had become afraid to be that visible, to stand out from the crowd. He was aware of Michael watching him, and he spoke rather slowly as he thought about what he wanted to say.

'I do know that I'm not using all my talents and abilities, probably nowhere near it. But what I've also just realized is that somewhere along the way I have settled for less than the best for myself.' Tom wasn't looking at Michael: his eyes were fixed on the ceiling over his head as if he was looking for the right answer. 'I thought that if I just stayed where I was then I could reduce the stress I was feeling, but instead I got more and more pressured. I haven't let myself move out of my comfort zone for years, and I think I got into the habit of not looking to the future because I didn't like what I could see there: myself in the same job, year after year.' Tom unfolded his arms and stretched them out in front of him as if he was trying to push away that unwelcome vision of his future.

Michael offered a sympathetic nod but wanted to press Tom even harder to face what it was that had been holding him back.

'Let me tell you another little secret Tom, and that is that the way to push out of your comfort zone is to face your fears and limiting beliefs. Now, I have been a runner most of my life and I'm going to run a marathon in three days' time. Do you think most men my age would believe they could do that?'

Tom had no real idea how old Michael was, but he certainly had to be nearing sixty although he looked fit and trim. 'I guess not', he said.

'Exactly' Michael said. 'They believe that they can't do it, so actually they are right. You know the old saying 'whether you believe you can, or whether you believe you can't – you're right.' It was Henry Ford who started the Ford Motor Company who said that, and he knew a thing or two about being successful. If you accept as a limiting belief that you can't run marathons all your life, then you won't get onto the starting line. Now I know I'm not going to finish first, but *I believe* I will finish and I don't allow myself to think any other way. I'm ready to keep testing my limits, move myself right out of my comfort zone, because that's when I can be really proud of who I am. Sitting at home watching it on TV isn't the same thing! Now let's hear it, what is your limiting belief?'

Tom spoke almost without thought, as if he needed to say it fast before he lost the courage to say it at all.

'When I played tennis, I always believed I would win and I usually did. For some time though, I seem to have been losing confidence, I'm not sure if I have that winning streak any more.'

Michael let him sit in silence for a moment, then when it was clear Tom wasn't going to say any more he gently said to him, 'Tom, if you had what it takes to be a winner then, you have it now. What you are faced with is a belief that you no longer can do it. All the things that made you a winner then are still with you. What you have to do is rediscover them, and sure it might be uncomfortable, painful even, to force yourself to really test your limits again, but until you are willing to stand up and be counted you won't know what it is you are capable of.'

As Tom thought about that, Olivia came through from the galley with an armful of newspapers and magazines. She came to Tom first, although it was to both of them that she spoke. 'I know you want all of them Mr Redford, but what about you sir?'

As Michael reached forward she gave him three newspapers and two magazines, one of each that she carried. Tom shook his head as he felt he had enough to think about without adding in the day's news! As she moved on and Michael slid the papers into the briefcase at his feet, Tom asked him 'Are you really going to get through all of those?'

'Of course' replied Michael 'it's all part of extending your comfort zone.'

Tom laughed, 'I wouldn't have thought like that. How is that going to stretch someone like you, except in the time it will take you to read them?'

Michael surprised him by not answering straight away, but changing tack once again.

'I notice that you never answered my question about how much of your potential you are using, but I hope you're still thinking about it because you're going to have to answer that question for yourself if not for me. Don't discount the incredible knowledge we can all get from reading, because it's one of the best ways to increase that potential. *I believe* that in order to make the most of who you are then you have to stretch one of the greatest muscles in the body – and that's your brain. Knowledge is power, you need to know what's going on in the world, and you need to have your views challenged. As you well know the whole world is now accessible to us, through travel and through the internet. There is so much opportunity for knowledge and it's available to you twenty four seven; you just have to open your mind and find it. For instance, don't just read the newspaper that agrees with your take on the world – how is that going to move you out of your comfort zone? You know I said you should do something every day that makes you uncomfortable?'

Tom nodded in agreement and tried to figure out what was coming next.

'Well,' Michael continued. 'You also have to do something every day to sow a seed of opportunity. Something that moves you on towards your goal, and all successful entrepreneurs are always looking for an edge, an advantage. That usually comes from being open to new information and often from the most unlikely sources. I might read a newspaper article about a guy who is trying to develop a new product for large scale construction work for say, hospitals, but he can't get the government interested. Now it might be that I have overseas interests where we have to build hospitals as part of our development plan and I can see that it might benefit me to get in touch with him. Now I might have found out about him anyway, but maybe not in time to make him an offer before somebody else gets in. That is my seed. Now what seeds are you sowing?'

Tom thought, and then said, 'To begin with I'm reading Napoleon Hill, and I have met you and started taking notes!'

Michael reached down and picked up one of the newspapers. 'OK, so you think some more about it and I'll see if there are any new challenges waiting for me in here.'

He switched on the overhead reading light, opened the newspaper and began to read as Tom started writing in the notebook to make sure he hadn't missed anything.

TOM'S NOTES

I B(E)LIEVE –
EXTEND YOUR COMFORT ZONE

- You must face your fears and limiting beliefs
  head-on to develop your self-belief.
- Whether you believe you can, or believe
  you can't, you are right (Henry Ford).
- You must do one thing each day which
  makes you feel uncomfortable.
- You must sow a seed of opportunity every day.

Chapter Three

As Tom glanced through his notes, he was aware that around him on the plane people were getting on with everyday things like dozing with their headrests back, reading newspapers or books, and the woman across the aisle was manicuring her nails a vibrant red and bouncing her foot to the rhythm that only she could hear through her headphones. Normally Tom would have been checking his notes for the meeting, worrying if he'd missed anything or taking the opportunity to get a bit of extra rest. Now, he felt different. Somehow more aware of what was going on around him, more engaged with the future and not just his immediate tasks. Reality had somehow changed and he was really starting to see things differently. He wasn't sure where he was going, but he knew it was a journey he was ready to take.

'I really can't believe my luck' he thought. *'This is just what I needed'*. Seeing that Michael was still reading, Tom stood up and stretched his arms over his head, rolled his shoulders and decided to take a walk. He set off up the aisle and as he passed through from business to economy class he could see that the entire plane was full, there was not one spare seat to be had anywhere. Where he had been sitting had been quiet, and very comfortable. Here there was a lot more noise, the underlying hum of the engines, the rise and fall of conversations and yet he didn't feel irritated by it like he usually did. He was grateful for the chance that had moved him up to travel at the sharp end of the plane and thought that the attendant at the gate had been absolutely right when he said he had the second best seat. Being in 1B really was a much better way to travel!

As he strolled up the carpeted aisle he was observing what was going on around him, but in his head he was still engaged with what Michael had told him. He could see that *I believe* was something that he too might be able to use to make the break that he had been thinking of for so long. When he reached the back of the plane he saw the stewardesses preparing to bring a drinks trolley back towards him, so he turned around and headed back to his seat.

Michael glanced up as he arrived and smiled as he saw Tom take his notebook out of his jacket pocket. 'Well, I can see you are ready to start again!' he said.

'Only if you are' replied Tom. 'I have been thinking about what you have said and thinking how lucky I was to be sitting here.'

'You believe in luck?' Michael asked him.

Tom sized him up, wondering if he was being serious. 'Of course I do – it's luck that makes all the difference between success and failure. I was lucky to get the seat next to you. Without that I wouldn't be having this conversation.'

Michael drew a large tick in the air with his finger. 'Yet again you've hit on one of the elements of *I believe!*'

Tom laughed. 'Now that may have been luck. So it is luck, after all, that is the "L" in *I believe,* isn't it?'

'It is certainly one of them' agreed Michael, 'but not in the way that you probably think. Luck can't be discounted, of course, but it also can't be relied upon. No successful entrepreneur makes a fortune by relying on luck alone. You have to make it work for you.'

Tom was looking puzzled. 'You don't think it was lucky that I was sitting in the one seat on the plane next to the man that could help me see how to move forward?'

'No I don't' replied Michael, 'and let me tell you why. Yes you got the seat next to me, but that was no guarantee that we would have this conversation. What was it do you think that started the ball rolling?'

As Tom continued to look unsure, Michael helped him out. 'It was my seeing that you were reading *Think and Grow Rich* that started it all. I was intrigued to see you reading it and that told me something about you. It told me that you were looking to make your life better and were prepared to stretch out to reach it. Now you may call that luck, but if you hadn't already bought that book and started to read it I probably wouldn't have taken the same notice of you. You remember that I said to you how important it was to sow a seed of opportunity every day?' As Tom nodded, he continued 'well that book was your seed for today. You create your own luck by networking with influential people and that book, and your decision to read it, gave you that opportunity. Do you agree?'

Tom nodded. 'In theory yes, but I have a question for you. Wasn't it luck that it was you sitting next to me and not someone who wouldn't have been interested in what I read?'

Michael shook his head firmly. 'You could look at it that way, but in my view luck is the crossroads where opportunity and preparation meet. In order to get to that crossroads you need to create opportunities and do all the right preparation. If you do that, then you could say you're going to be more lucky than most. But if you don't create those conditions even if you get a lucky break you won't be prepared to really exploit its potential to the full. If a great business opportunity comes along but you haven't done your homework, and know all the angles inside out of what you are going in to, then all the luck in the world won't help you pull it off.' He pointed at Tom's notebook. 'From your notes in there, you will see that we have already talked about how important it is that you continue to learn, read, ask questions, watch trends, and think of how to create connections that only you can see through your map of the world. You don't find opportunities by sitting at home watching TV and you don't make a million by being lucky – the harder you work the more you create your own luck.' Michael watched Tom's face as he absorbed what he had been hearing. 'What I'm saying is that you can't rely on it. You have to keep sowing those seeds every day and see which ones come up. In life good follows bad, things go in cycles, and you have to keep going no matter what. Think of how farmers approach their business. Every year they sow their seeds and they don't know in advance which seeds will grow and which will fail, which year will be a great harvest and which a terrible one. Whatever the outcome, they go on year after year persistently sowing those seeds. You see, there is such a thing as cause and effect going on here. You told me that you have been reading business development books for quite a while and that nothing has happened; well actually you were like the farmer and finally this seed has come good. But if you had got disheartened and stopped buying and reading those kinds of books then we wouldn't be talking together now. Now do you get it?'

'Yes I do, and I'm really glad I did keep on going' Tom finally responded. 'I just always thought that very successful people had more luck than I did. But what you are saying is that they worked harder to make the luck happen. I'm no stranger to hard work though. In my job I couldn't do any more than I do now and yet that lucky break still eludes me.'

Michael's look let him know that he still hadn't got it: 'Now look Tom – you have to stop thinking as an employee. This is not about your job; it's about how you approach your life, your future. You need to start thinking like an entrepreneur and that means focusing on what you're passionate about, what you want to change in your life and being totally honest with yourself about what you really want. Luck is only one of the elements of the "L" in *I believe*. The other "L" is lies, because to be a successful entrepreneur means there is absolutely no room for lying.'

Feeling a bit stung, Tom quickly retorted 'Are you saying I'm dishonest?'

'No, at least not in the way you think. What I'm asking is how honest you are with yourself about what you want and what you are prepared to do to get it. Believe me Tom, I'm not questioning your general honesty, just asking you to realistically look at how much time, energy and commitment you are willing to give in order to create lasting success. It's not about lying to the world, and telling them that you are definitely on course to achieving your goals. It's about being totally, brutally, honest with yourself and knowing when you are really telling the truth and when you are making excuses, because actually you are not one hundred per cent committed to making it happen. Entrepreneurs have to be honest with themselves if they want to create lasting success. It's about your personal integrity and that's something you don't want to compromise if you want to be true to yourself.'

Tom had been leaning forward to catch every word, and now he let out a breath and sat back. He knew Michael wasn't attacking him, just making him really question himself. He had not been forced to think so much about himself and what he really wanted for many years, and although it felt strange, it also felt good. 'I hope I'm completely up for it. I never realized how much I wanted things to be different until I started talking to you.'

'I hate to tell you this Tom, but hoping for it to happen just isn't enough. You know we shape our destiny by our decisions. Taking the attitude of 'what will be, will be' is not what successful entrepreneurs do. They know what they want and they go about making it happen by taking dramatic action, and lots of it. It's another old cliché, but still true, that life is not a rehearsal. You don't get a second chance to polish it and make it right. You just have to take a risk and go for it. Hope won't do it for you. You're the one responsible for making it happen, and if you stay true to yourself and treat others with respect and trust, then you reap what you sow. What you put out there always comes back, so you need to really think about what impact your thoughts and actions will have.'

'OK, I can see that, and I'm totally willing to do what I have to do to make things happen.' Tom sounded eager, but still not completely sure that he understood how to move forward with it. 'What do you think is the biggest change I need to make?'

Michael thought for a minute. 'Get into the good habit of being totally honest with yourself about what you are doing and why you're doing it. Don't let yourself worry if nothing seems to be happening immediately, just keep on being positive and doing all you can to network and leverage your opportunities. Out of those habits you can create the opportunity to make yourself into that entrepreneur that I think you really want to be.'

'It's really about committing to myself and my idea, isn't it?'

'Yes' Michael agreed. 'That, and realizing that **Lies and luck don't work**.'

'So what does work?' Tom wanted to get to the bottom of it.

'Well, you will just have to wait and see.' Michael gestured to the aisle where Olivia was approaching them with menus tucked under her arm. 'Looks like we have to think about what we want to eat, and you have some notes to write up, don't you?'

Tom turned to a new page and started to gather his thoughts.

TOM'S NOTES

I BE(L)IEVE —
LIES AND LUCK DON'T WORK
Luck

- Entrepreneurs create their own luck.
- Luck is the crossroads of
  preparation and opportunity.
- The harder you work, the luckier you become.
- You must read, ask questions, watch
  trends and network to create luck.
- New opportunities do not come from sitting
  at home watching TV — you need to
  get out and create lucky breaks.
- Remember cause and effect (you must
  sow the seeds of opportunity every day
  to reap the benefit in the future).

Lies

- You must be brutally honest with
  yourself as an entrepreneur.
- The only excuses are the ones you tell yourself.
- Hope is not good enough — action
  is what matters.
- You must have personal honesty, integrity,
  respect and trust — you cannot build
  lasting success without it.

Chapter Four

Olivia passed down the aisle handing out menus, and Tom tucked his in the side of his seat wanting to make sure he had written his notes out clearly. Michael had talked about the eight principles or insights that went into making *I believe* and he was beginning to get a glimpse of how it might all slot together. For the first time he could see a path opening up before him, and each of the ideas Michael had talked about were like stepping stones leading from one to the next. He bent over his notebook, making adjustments to what he had written, and marking comments next to things that had particularly struck him. He wasn't aware of Michael studying him as he wrote or that Michael was making mental notes of how well Tom was absorbing what he had said.

Olivia had already arrived back to take their orders. Startled, Tom looked up, then shook his head and smiled up at her. 'Sorry, I was miles away. I'll have a look now.' He put his notebook down and retrieved the menu.

'No problem, I'll be back in a couple of minutes' said Olivia as she walked on past them to the galley.

Michael had already laid his menu on his knee as if he had made up his mind. Tom was still looking at the menu when Michael spoke to him.

'You seemed very absorbed just then?'

'Yes' replied Tom. 'I'm beginning to see a pattern of where you might be leading me – but don't worry, I'm prepared for a few detours on the way!'

Michael laughed. 'I'll try and avoid detours, but I'm glad you're finding what we are talking about useful. Each of the separate principles of *I believe* is important on its own, but it's when you put them all together and rigorously apply them that you will really see change happening. There is no self-made millionaire that I know, and I've met quite a few, that doesn't operate from these principles – though they may not all describe them in the same way.' He nodded towards the menu that Tom had quickly glanced at and let fall to his lap as he listened. 'If you have made your mind up, then are you ready to move on to the next principle?'

Tom closed the menu and tapped the cover with his finger before he gave Michael his full attention. 'I'm certainly ready, but this time I don't think I'll even attempt to guess what it might be.'

'Well, for anyone working in business, and particularly with how you have described your job to me, this should be straightforward' said Michael.

Tom relaxed back into his seat. 'OK, you hooked me in again, what is it?'

'In a sense it's one you might think you know already, but I guess I'm going to ask you to think about it a little more deeply,' said Michael.

This really got Tom's interest and he barely registered Olivia returning to collect the menus. Her voice was asking what he wanted, and he quickly mentioned the first thing he remembered. As Tom had come to expect, Michael gave her his order rather more calmly. He was impressed by Tom's eagerness to get on and didn't want to make him wait too long. 'OK, we have a bit of time before our food arrives, so let's examine the next part of *I believe*. The "I" stands for **Install goals**, and it is almost like you need to hardwire your goals into your system so that they are running 24/7. It's about programming your subconscious so that the aware-ness of your goals, and what you have to do to achieve them, is a permanent programme that will keep prompting you to action. Trust me on this, Tom – if you don't pay real attention to your goals, nothing that you want to achieve is ever going to happen.'

Tom thought that sounded a bit excessive but he was will-ing to hear a bit more; after all, Michael had come up with the goods so far.

'I guess you are familiar with the concept of setting goals?' Michael enquired.

'Sometimes it feels like I have nothing else but goals,' sighed Tom. 'A list as long as your arm, all relating to work, and most of them unachievable – at least not in the time-frame my boss sets.'

'Sounds like mostly externally applied goals to me. The things your boss wants you to achieve, targets you have to get, sure they are all part of a normal business life but that's not what I'm talking about. I want you to think outside that employee mindset and move forward to thinking like an entrepreneur.' Michael thought for a minute and went on 'it's important that your goals have real meaning for you and that it's you who sets them, not someone else. To be a success-ful entrepreneur you go back to that passion, that great idea and create a clear vision of what you want to achieve. And nothing gets achieved unless you have clearly defined goals and a defined plan of action. Let me give you an example. Nowadays, space travel is taken for granted, but that very first step man took on the moon's surface was the most incredible thing any of us could imagine. And it only happened because the USA had a clear goal to get a man on the moon – not a vague statement about space exploration or investigating other galaxies, but a clear statement of intent. The then US President, John F. Kennedy, in a speech to Congress in 1961 made it crystal clear. He said, 'I believe that this nation should commit itself to achieving the goal, before this decade is out, of landing a man on the moon and returning him safely to the Earth.' He set the intention, stated when it should be done by and it was realized when Neil Armstrong's foot hit the surface. Now that is setting a goal and achieving it.'

Tom was too young to remember the landing, but he knew it had made history, and his own parents still talked about it as a landmark event in their lives. 'That was a major event, something to be inspired by certainly, but when I think about goals I usually just see them as part of my everyday working life, and frankly just something to be got through as fast as possible.' He hesitated, and Michael nodded, encouraging him to go on. 'I suppose my experience of goals is that they always seem like a moving target and not something that I am choosing. More like "get this one done and move on to the next thing". I can't think about the big picture, I'm too busy doing the next item on the list.'

'Again, you are thinking like an employee. Those goals are not taking you anywhere you want to go, because they are not your personal goals and they are not serving your bigger vision. There are some basic rules around setting goals.'

Tom interrupted him. 'Oh, yes I know all about that!'

Michael shook his head gently and chose his words carefully. 'You may know it, but I suspect you don't know why it's so important. The way I see it, with any goals you need three things: a why, a what, and a how. The *why* is the motivation, why you really want to achieve this, the *what* is the goal itself, and the *how* is the method that will get you there. Let's go back to that example of the moon landing. Tell me what you think is the why.'

Tom shrugged his shoulders. 'My father always thought it was because the USA wanted to prove that they had the technology and needed to get there before anyone else. The first nation to get to the moon, that was really something, nobody remembers who came second but everyone knows it was Neil Armstrong of the USA who got there first. So I guess it was that desire to be the first, national pride maybe?'

'That was definitely one of the motivators. You know all about the desire to be first, you talked about how great it felt to win a tennis match, so tell me, is that a great motivator for a goal?'

Tom nodded his agreement and Michael continued. 'The *what* is easy because we know it was to get a man on the moon, so now tell me about the how.'

'A heck of a lot of money, research and trial and error I imagine!' responded Tom, and as Michael looked set to help him out, Tom went on 'but that's not what you want me to say! I do see that they had to have a great vision and then break it down into actions that led them to that final goal. The money, the research, the years of work are all about the same thing aren't they, being focused on that goal?'

'Absolutely,' agreed Michael. 'They were willing to set a huge, unbelievable goal and dream the undreamable. Something that had only been seen in comic books became a reality. Because they stretched their horizons they found a way to make it happen.' He gestured out of the window of the plane. 'Do you think we could be sitting here comfortably moving above the earth if the Wright brothers hadn't set a goal to fly?'

'I guess none of my goals have been big enough, or what I wanted enough. I go through the motions, but that big goal has always eluded me.' Tom was reflective and Michael gave him a minute before he replied.

'Tom, I promise you that if you have a definite outcome you're working towards, then the mind at the subconscious level does everything it can to make it a reality. What we direct our thoughts towards – what we think about – produces our reality because thoughts are things. Believe me, if you can conceive it, you can achieve it. Now, let me ask you something. This big goal that you have in mind, are you really clear about why you want it, and what exactly it is?'

'No, I guess it's something around being successful, working for myself, but the details aren't really clear yet, though I feel somehow closer to that after talking with you.'

Michael drummed his fingers on the armrest as he thought about how to help Tom. 'First you need to make finding your business idea a clear goal, then your subconscious will get to work on producing ideas for you. Just asking your subconscious doesn't do it. You must make it a definite goal otherwise you have very little chance of achieving it.' Tom was making a quick note, so Michael paused for a moment before going on. 'Now there are some simple practical steps around goals that you need to follow. Tell me, when you have tried to achieve big goals in the past, have you made them clear and written them out? Were they time-based, so you had a real deadline in mind? Did you have a defined plan of action? And most importantly, did you review your written goals daily?'

Tom had been absorbed in what Michael was saying and slowly he shook his head. 'Lots of questions, but I guess yes and no. I can see that I never followed any kind of plan really and although I wrote my goals down I only looked at them occasionally.'

'Writing your goals down and reading them at least once a day is how you programme your subconscious mind to achieve them. It's like a silent message that is transmitted, heard and acted upon. Just having a goal, but not writing it down, reduces your chance of achieving it. In my book a goal unwritten is just a wish.' Michael was watching Tom to see what his reaction was to what he was telling him.

'I always knew it was important to have goals, but you are saying that they are crucial to achieve any real sort of success.' Tom underlined what he had written in his notebook.

'Absolutely, you need to see your finished goal in your mind, and then write down what you want in less than ten words. Then keep that written goal in your wallet and look at it frequently throughout the day so you're keeping it right at the front of your consciousness. That keeps you focused and that is fundamental to success. Without focus you will just drift, waste your energy and end up wandering aimlessly. Think of it this way. Goals are dreams with deadlines, and it's the deadline that makes it real. It's as simple as the fact that if you don't know what you want, you will never get it.'

'So focusing on my goals will keep me focused on that main passion, that dream, and that's how I will get there.' Tom wrote down goals and focus.

'Yes,' said Michael. 'Now you are looking to the future, and beyond your next monthly salary payment. You and I got talking because you had a copy of Napoleon Hill's book *Think and Grow Rich*; well, here's a great quote from it that I learned many years ago and have written down and carried in my wallet ever since. Read it out.' He took out a thin black leather wallet and removed a folded and worn piece of paper and handed it to Tom who unfolded it and Michael listened as he read it aloud. 'There is one quality that one must possess to win, and that is definiteness of purpose, the knowledge of what one wants, and a burning desire to possess it.'*[Think and Grow Rich, Chapter 2 – Napoleon Hill, 1937.]*

Tom looked thoughtful and handed the paper back to Michael who returned it to his wallet and carried on where he had left off. 'To make your goals really happen Tom, you need to take that to heart, not just read it, but really live it. When it comes to achieving what you want I have found there are four clear stages.' He held up his left hand and tapped his fingers in turn as he listed them. 'First is stage one, your dreams, your vision, how they need to become specific goals. Those goals are stage two and they lead you to stage three as you work out what steps you need to take to achieve that goal. Next is stage three where those steps lead you to devise specific tasks to achieve them. Finally you are at stage four where you are turning those tasks into action items. Together they all create a plan for you to achieve that dream, that goal. Let me give you a real example, from your own experience of getting to the airport to catch this flight. Your mind was working towards a definite major outcome. You were absolutely clear that you needed to be here on time and your mind would not give up on the goal that you should and would make the plane. When you were waiting at that gate I bet you had only one purpose in mind and that was to make the flight. Am I right?' Tom nodded his agreement and Michael went on. 'It is that singleness of purpose, that single-minded approach that is needed as an entrepreneur. Once you set the goal of making this flight then all the actions in between are steps to get you to that definite outcome of being on this plane.'

Tom could follow Michael's train of thought, but wasn't sure that his own goals were going to be that easy to break down. He sighed and tapped the point of his pen against the open page of his notebook. 'It's just that my goals seem unattainable right now and I'm not sure how I deal with that.'

Surprisingly, Michael was enthusiastic about this potentially negative statement. 'Unattainable goals are great: they force you to think differently. Do you think that those scientists who worked on the space project in the early days thought that it was possible to put a man on the moon? No, they didn't but they went ahead anyway and discovered new ways to achieve space travel. They had to be creative and inventive and discard what they already knew for what they now needed to know. And they were the people who had to find that solution. It's truly amazing what the human mind can achieve with total focus and concentration. Of course, it took years, but they saw that goal through to the end, and although the action they had to take was massive, it started with them deciding to go for that goal and moving forward one step at a time. What they had to do was start with the end in mind – the man on the moon – and work back to the beginning to see how to achieve it. It's the same for all of us. Once you know what the desired goal is, you see it clearly and then work back to a place where you can start to take action.'

'That's a lot of focus and concentration', Tom observed.

'Yes, it is, but it can also be great fun. I bet those people at NASA really enjoyed the journey on the way, the experience of being at the cutting edge of so many new ideas and technologies. All the things they discovered that may not have contributed directly to that first space landing but which had applications to industry and people's lives in ways they couldn't have imagined. It's not just about the goal; it's about enjoying the highs and lows on the way there. It's about being passionate about life, not just being a spectator.'

'I never thought of goals like that – for me they were just another part of the daily grind. Now you make them sound more like an epic hero's journey!'

'I guess, in a way there are similarities.' The sound of a trolley alerted him to look towards the galley where he could see Olivia coming through the doorway with a couple of trays in her hands. 'Well our hero's journey is going to have to wait a while, as it looks like lunch is on the way.'

'I'm going to write a few quick notes before I eat while it's still fresh in my mind.' Tom ducked his head down and began to write as Olivia passed a tray to Michael.

TOM'S NOTES

I BEL(I)EVE – INSTALL GOALS

- You must have clearly defined written goals
  that you are constantly working towards.
- You must review your goals daily – and
  make sure you still have the passion, belief
  and motivation to achieve them.
- You need to break larger goals down
  into smaller steps – and create a
  plan of action to achieve them.
- Goals should be a stretch and almost unachievable
  – think big, think of landing a man on the moon.
- Written goals programme your subconscious
  mind like no other tool – this is vital.
- A goal is a dream with a deadline.

Chapter Five

Tom leaned back in his seat with a contented smile on his face. 'That was the best food I have ever had on a plane. No matter what you say Michael, the fringe benefits of being a millionaire entrepreneur are definitely worth while!' He stretched his arms above his head and couldn't stop himself from yawning. 'The only problem is it makes me sleepy.'

'In that case, let's get some more coffee, as you are about to discover the next key part of *I believe!*' Michael reached up to the bell over his head and pushed his own plate aside as he waited for Olivia to respond.

'Don't tell me I have to give up sleep,' exclaimed Tom, only half joking.

'No, not entirely but a little-known fact about entrepreneurs is that they only work half days!' Anticipating Tom's likely interruption he went on with a twinkle in his eye 'and as a day is 24 hours, they only work half of that!' In fact, most dedicated entrepreneurs will work day and night on a venture or project to see it through to completion.'

Michael nodded as Olivia came down the aisle towards them. Michael asked her for some coffee for the two of them and she picked up their plates and went back to the galley.

'You want to make sure I stay awake, don't you?' Tom joked.

Laughing, Michael returned to his theme. 'Tom, you have got to be fully awake to take advantage of the opportunities that come your way. So yes, I want you focused on what I'm telling you. We don't want you to drift into that employee mindset again, but to start applying some of the insights we've talked about so you're automatically thinking like a millionaire.'

Tom could see he was very serious about this, and so he nodded and turned to give him his full attention as Michael leaned forward to emphasize his point. 'The next letter of *I believe* is "E" and that stands for **Enjoy hard work.** It is essential for you to understand that, just like you have to pay interest on a loan or debt, there is a price to pay for success. To be a really successful entrepreneur you need to work around 80 hours a week, and the harder you work the more successful you are. Do you really think that's just a coincidence?'

'No, they always say hard work brings its own reward. And I certainly work hard, so I already have that principle under my belt!' Tom was confident that here at least was something he already knew about and was putting into practice daily. He waited for Michael to continue as Olivia returned and poured them each a cup of coffee. Michael stirred his for a few seconds before replying.

'Well, like all the other principles we have already talked about, it's one thing to think you know what they are and quite another to actually live them. Sure you work hard, but for someone else. Now cast your mind back and remember the difference between how you feel now and how you felt when you were playing tennis. Did you put in plenty of hours of practice?'

Tom shrugged and then took a sip of coffee. 'Of course, you don't win without putting in the time and effort on the practice court, but that was different.'

'How?' asked Michael.

'Well, for one thing I so much wanted to win, that the hours I put in weren't a problem. And for another, I loved doing it.'

Pleased with Tom's insights, Michael took a mouthful of coffee before he went on. 'The great English playwright Noel Coward summed it up very well when he said that "work is more fun than fun". He had this image of being a real party animal, always at first nights and glamorous events, but the reality was that he worked incredibly hard every single day to produce the sheer volume of work that he did. At the time people thought he threw off his plays without any effort, but when his biography came out it became clear that he had spent the majority of every day writing. He never put it second to any other activity and that's how he could produce so much work. He was only able to do that because it was totally his passion. When you love doing something it is never hard work.'

Tom was never sure where Michael was going to lead him next. Quoting Noel Coward was not something he had expected from a businessman, but he was coming to realize that Michael was open to all kinds of information and influences. 'Well, yes, but creative people have to have that passion don't they? I guess it's what drives them to produce the work they do. It's different for them.'

'No, it's exactly the same. It isn't just creative people Tom. Being a successful entrepreneur means you have the same drive, the same passion. If you don't have that you are not going to be willing to do all the things that are necessary, you won't be prepared to work those 80 hours a week and keep yourself focused exclusively on achieving your goals. Without that passion, and willingness to work hard and enjoy it, you won't have the self-discipline to turn your winning business idea into a commercial success.'

Both men had now finished their coffee, and as Olivia passed down the aisle with a fresh pot, they held their cups up for a refill. Tom was turning over in his mind what Michael had just said. He was beginning to realize that here was someone who really practised what he preached, and he wanted to know more about how he had become that way. 'This dedication to hard work, is it something you developed or did it come naturally?'

Michael took a moment to consider. 'I guess you could say it's always been there. I told you my family were market traders, and that's a job where you put in very long hours, so it was in the blood, so to speak. I worked after school with my uncle on most days so that habit of hard work was developed, though I would have to say my two older brothers never had the same interest I did in putting in any extra hours, even for more pocket money! My incentive to work hard was to pursue my passion for running and get the best possible trainers I could to help me do that. From there it expanded because I found it so interesting and all-consuming that, like you with your tennis, I happily spent all my time on it. Once I started selling to my school friends and then got my own market stall I was hooked. I couldn't think of a better way to spend my days than pursuing my passion so I ended up working at least 12 hours a day, and often more. Like I said, it's not hard work when you really enjoy it. Look at what we have already talked about in *I believe*. Those principles of being passionate, having a burning desire to achieve and total inner belief around a clear goal are all essential. But let me ask you this: how can you make all that happen if you aren't prepared to put in the hours? And why would you not enjoy working hard for something you want so much?'

Tom could see the sense in what Michael was saying. 'I know I said earlier that I was used to hard work, but what you're saying is something different. That if I'm enjoying it, it won't seem like hard work, whereas now I do often work long hours but I resent it because it's doing things I'm not that interested in. That's really what we're talking about here, right?'

'Exactly. Now just imagine what you could achieve by working in exactly the same way, but focused on your own goals and desires. Wouldn't that be something you would be happy doing?'

As Michael picked up his cup again, Tom felt he had got hold of a valuable idea here and wanted to pursue it. 'Like I said, everyone believes that hard work brings its own rewards, so why aren't more people successful?'

Michael laughed. 'Because as I keep saying, knowing or believing something and actually doing it are two very different things. Of course you must put the hours in to be successful, but you must also be prepared to make sacrifices too. Self-discipline is very important here and you have to be ready to sometimes do things that you just don't want to do. Remember, I said there was a price to pay for success? Well, working long hours means you may have to choose to do one thing over another. You can't be at an important business meeting in New York and at the men's singles finals in Wimbledon at the same time. You have to choose and although you could see it as a sacrifice not to be at the sports event you are simply choosing to do something that's more important to you. Something you love to do and have the complete belief that you can make happen, that's your choice. Once you have put those written goals in place, that we talked about before lunch, you will be checking on them daily and that energy and focus will open up more opportunities for you. Opportunities that you can't afford to let slip by. You can't let yourself drift mentally. You have to stay completely focused. But if you are doing what you love it's not hard work: it's as natural as breathing.'

He watched as Tom made a few notes and then went on. 'When I was talking about opportunities, there's something else I wanted to mention – it's vital that you are ready to seize the moment. You can't afford to procrastinate and delay before taking action. We talked a while ago about planting seeds of opportunity; well, you also have to be ready to seize those opportunities the moment they are ripe. If you're prepared to enjoy hard work you'll be in the right place to keep creating opportunities, but you need to keep hustling for them. Putting a lot of energy behind what you do will create those opportunities, for sure, but you also have to be ready to take immediate action to get the results you want.'

'My father always told me that good things come to those who wait, but I don't think you'd agree with that, would you?' said Tom.

'To be honest I've always thought that's something said by people who don't want to put the energy into making things happen,' replied Michael. 'In fact, I would go further and say that people who wait are only getting what is left by those who hustle! If you really want to use a common phrase, try "the early bird catches the worm!"'

'OK, I get it.' Tom flipped over the page of his notebook and quickly wrote a few words. 'I got on this plane thinking I would have a quick bite to eat, look over some of my notes and then snooze. Now I'm full of ideas and plans for what else I could be doing with my life and I don't want to waste any of the time I have available here.' He looked a little surprised at what he had just said, and then added 'what I'm really saying is that yes, I'm enjoying myself and you're right – it doesn't feel like work at all.'

'I'm really glad to hear it,' said Michael and he picked up the newspaper again while Tom turned to his notebook.

TOM'S NOTES

I BELI(E)VE — ENJOY HARD WORK

- Success is simple — but not easy!
  You must enjoy hard work.
- Successful entrepreneurs work around 80
  hours a week — it is this level of effort
  that is required to create lasting success.
- Work must be fun — but if you do something
  you love, believe in, and are motivated
  by, the necessary hard work becomes
  easier (and doesn't feel like work).
- You must have the self-discipline to
  do the things you do not want to do,
  when you do not want to do them.
- Entrepreneurs must make sacrifices — although
  a better definition of this is 'making choices'
  which take you closer to your goal.
- Successful entrepreneurs immerse
  themselves in their business.
- Time is the most precious resource
  — procrastination is the thief of time.
- Must have urgency as an entrepreneur. Good
  things come to those who wait — but only
  what is left behind by those who hustle.

Chapter Six

Michael had finished with his newspaper and was glancing through the in-flight magazine while Tom finished writing up his notes. Underlining a few key points he sat back poised for the next instalment. Michael looked deep in thought and Tom coughed gently to indicate he was ready to continue.' I was just thinking about my own career', ventured Michael. 'To many I guess it looks like plain sailing.' Tom smiled. 'I wouldn't say plain sailing, but like many successful entrepreneurs part of your skill is making it look easy.' 'Yes and I accept that,' said Michael, 'my businesses have been really successful, I'm proud to say. People often credit me with having "the magic touch" or owning some great secret that allows me to be successful where others have failed. You know it wasn't easy and I don't believe I have a so-called 'magic touch', but I do think there's a secret, and I think anyone can find it.' Tom second-guessed him: 'And that secret is the principles of *I believe* that we've been speaking about, right?' 'Without a doubt,' agreed Michael, 'my own journey has always been accompanied by the principles of *I believe*. Over the years I have developed and refined them to keep myself on track for success. It's been a journey of constant challenges and opportunities won and lost.

Keen to show Michael just how significant this conversation was, Tom interjected: 'I already feel excited about applying the principles we've talked about, Michael, I really feel like I'm benefiting from your experience.' Satisfied that Tom had fully grasped the importance of these principles he continued: 'Well, the next principle is perhaps the most hidden secret of all and the one that is absolutely crucial for success. The next part of *I believe* is absolutely the one thing that you cannot afford to be without if you want to be a successful entrepreneur.'

Tom had started to close his notebook, ready to pay attention, but when he heard those words he kept it open and looked back at Michael. 'Everything you have said so far makes perfect sense, so I'm all ears to find out what the next one is!' He looked down at the page and appeared to be recapping to himself. 'OK, we had got to the second "E" of *I believe,* so it has to be "V" next.'

'It certainly is, care to take a guess at what it might be?'

Tom laughed, 'Well, let's face it, my guesses have been a bit off the mark so far. However, let's see; "V" could be victory, vanquish, valiant or vanity, though I don't think so somehow. I know, what about vision? That's certainly essential from all you have said so far.'

'Good choice, but not what I'm thinking of. It is what I'm sure is the most hidden characteristic of every successful entrepreneur.'

'Now this really is going to be interesting,' said Tom eagerly, 'I hope you're going to put me out of my misery?'

'Well, it stands for *very.* In fact double that, for very, very.' Michael was delighted to see the blank look on Tom's face.

'Very? No, there has to be more than that. Very, very what?'

Relenting, Michael explained. '**Very, very persistent**.' Tom looked a little disappointed as if he had expected something much more dramatic than this. 'You look unsure, but trust me on this one. If you were to choose just one part of your personality to develop that would virtually guarantee your success, I'd like you to put persistence at the top of your list.

You've only just started reading *Think and Grow Rich*, but you'll see that Napoleon Hill felt so strongly about this subject, that he devoted an entire chapter to it. Now, he studied many of the world's most successful people and he found that all of them had one quality that was lacking in those less successful than themselves. When he looked at people like Henry Ford and Thomas Edison he realized that the true secret of their success was that they were persistent, way beyond the average. Sure, they were also clever, resourceful and inventive, but if they hadn't also been very, very persistent you wouldn't know their names today.'

Tom wasn't sure that this really was the secret. 'You think it was just persistence that made them so successful? That's all?'

Michael nodded slowly. 'Well, there were other contributing factors, but just think about it. Look back at some of your accomplishments in the past – large and small – you would have to agree that persistence played an important role in your success, wouldn't you?'

Tom leaned his head back and scanned his memory for something that would be relevant to what Michael was saying, and the picture of him accepting a winner's medal for the university team flashed into his mind. 'Well, yes, you don't win tennis matches by quitting. I guess that's a kind of persistence, but why do you say it's the most hidden characteristic of successful entrepreneurs? To be honest it sounds like quite an obvious one.'

'I'll try and explain, and you mentioning tennis makes it easier because that is a sport where it's really laid out for you to see. How often have tournaments been won, not by the best player, but by the one who hung in and waited it out and kept chasing down every ball that came their way, no matter how hopeless it seemed? They could be two sets down and they just wouldn't quit, they still believed they could win. That's real persistence and that's how you get to be a champion. Yes, you practise for hours and work on your technique and passionately want to win, but if you aren't also very, very persistent you won't be successful. I say it's a hidden characteristic because what other people see is the surface stuff. They talk about talent and timing and luck, but what they don't realize is that none of that matters. Successful people aren't quitters. Go back to your tennis days. If you had given up when the game was going against you then how many matches would you have won?'

Tom's eyes sparkled with pleasure as he remembered his glory days on the court. 'I see where you're going with this. I wouldn't have won as many matches, that's for sure.'

'Yeah,' Michael agreed. 'Of course you don't win all of them, but if you don't keep trying then you will certainly lose a lot more. Most people just don't see it, but persistence is the single most important thing that makes the difference between success and failure.'

'So I don't have to be that much better than anyone else, I just have to keep going?' Tom was still not entirely convinced – this sounded too easy.

'Persistence is what is underlies all the other principles we've talked about. If you want to be successful, that kind of mental strength has to become a way of life and it starts from *I believe*. When you read back through your notes you'll see that. You have to want something so much that it becomes a heated desire … a passion in your belly. You must fall in love with that idea and totally immerse yourself in it so that your passion is present every day in each action that moves you towards your goal. At that point, persistence will be virtually automatic.'

'You make it sound like the glue that holds everything together, but up until now I have never really considered it to be so important to success,' Tom said, seeing it within the context of the other principles.

'Well, I can assure you that without persistence your plans will certainly not succeed! Persistence is a subject I have really studied and I can tell you one thing I know for certain: very few people ever, mentally or verbally, say to themselves "… this is what I really want and I'm prepared to give my life for it", and so they never develop the persistence to achieve it. Persistence is a unique mental strength and you'll need that to overcome all the obstacles and problems that you encounter in business. You have to learn to never accept no for an answer, you need to keep going until you get the final yes.'

'You know Michael, I'm not sure I have what it takes,' Tom said slowly. 'Will-power has never exactly been my strong point. Sometimes I have been more successful than others, but there have been lots of things I have started but not finished. I didn't stick it out to the end, so what does that say about me?'

'I don't think it says you have no will-power; plenty of people have a very strong will but they can still lack the persistence required to achieve their goals. Generally, in my experience, if someone lacks persistence, it's because they are putting effort and energy into a goal that they are not truly passionate about. In that case, there is no huge desire to pull them forward. Although will-power is important in moving you towards a goal, if there is ever a war between the will and the imagination, the imagination will win every time.'

Tom jumped in as he wasn't sure he was following this. 'Hang on a minute – how did we get to imagination? I thought we were talking about persistence?'

'We are, and we're also talking about all we've seen so far in *I believe*' Michael ticked them off on his fingers as he listed them out: 'Be passionate, extend your comfort zone, lies and luck, and installing goals – they're all linked by your persistence. When I talk about a war between the will and the imagination, what that means is that you're powered by desire and fuelled by the dream you hold. Once you start to use your imagination to help you build a bigger picture of your dream, to define and refine it until you get it just right in your mind, the emotion that is triggered by that desire far outweighs any force that may be caused by sheer will alone. It is easy to find people who are persistently doing what they don't want to do and achieving results that they don't want. A lack of persistence is not their problem. They are applying it to the wrong thing: to something they are not passionate about. Vision and desire have to be the focus of your attention if you're going to develop persistence into the great ally it can become.'

Tom had been listening intently and Michael could almost see his thoughts whizzing round his brain as he processed what was being said.

'So therefore, once I've found that source of my passion, my idea, it is persistence that will keep me going? I have been thinking about whether I had the talent or the ability to really succeed, but this means looking at what I really need in a very different way.'

'It does, doesn't it. If persistence is taken with the other qualities of the millionaire mindset, such as passion and self-belief, it can be an extremely powerful tool. Let me give you an example. The very first man to climb Everest and success-fully return was Sir Edmund Hillary in 1953, with his Sherpa guide Tenzing Norgay. Now Hillary had tried and failed to climb Everest in the previous two years, but he was absolutely immersed in his vision and desire to see himself standing on top of that great mountain. Whatever obstacles stood in his way he persistently kept going to overcome them, because he was emotionally involved with that image of himself. Of course, he was a courageous and a skilled climber, but with-out being tenacious and persistent he wouldn't have gone back for that third attempt.'

Tom had been unconsciously doodling a picture of a mountain in his notebook and Michael glanced down at it. He took his own pen out, and held his hand out for the note-book. Tom handed it over and watched as Michael added four crosses from the bottom of the mountain to the top and numbered them one to four then passed the book back. Tom looked at it for a moment and then gave an enquiring look.

'Those are the four steps that anyone can take to ensure they develop the persistence it takes to get to the top of the mountain.

1. Have a clearly defined goal that you believe in, you are passionate about and you have an intense desire to reach.
2. Create a clear plan that you can begin working on immediately and anchor this with immediate and constant action.
3. Immerse yourself in the achievement of your goal – many people will try and knock you off track; listen to them and learn from them, but remain focused on your ultimate objective.
4. Surround yourself with the talented people who share your belief and passion – and who can help you achieve your goal.'

As Tom wrote the four steps out, Michael wanted to really impress on him how important this quality was to his future success. 'Persistence is a formidable force. Simply put, it achieves results. Those who accomplish success are the ones who have the mental strength and stamina to keep going when others around them are giving up. Do you accept the importance of persistence in all of this now?'

Tom nodded. 'Yes I do. If you had asked me before this flight I probably would have said it wasn't that important, but I see now that it's all about determination and doggedness. Never quitting, never giving up.'

'Yes, it's the ability to stay focused, keep going, and never give up until you've achieved your desired outcome. It's a fundamental quality of winners. And, like I said earlier, it's about learning never to accept no for an answer.'

Tom had heard this said before but wanted to challenge him on it. 'But do you really mean never? Surely there are times when you have to accept that it really is no?'

'If you really love what you are doing, and believe you are right to be doing it, then why would you accept no for an answer?' Michael responded.

Tom gathered his thoughts: 'So what you're saying here is that they are passionate, almost obsessed by what they do. They live and breathe their work and they certainly don't understand if you say no, they just keep on until they wear you down.'

'Well, that's not the most effective way to achieve a yes,' laughed Michael. 'One thing you learn is that you have to be agile and flexible, creative even, when you are faced with a no. If somebody says no, find a different way to get to yes by breaking the rules or thinking differently, in fact do whatever it takes. Do you remember I told you I started out by selling trainers?' Tom nodded and Michael went on. 'Well, I was only 16, with no capital and no track record and none of the big suppliers would give me the time of day. I tried and tried, and then I started thinking how else I might get stock. I approached small shoe shops and offered to buy lines that weren't selling. I found out about bankrupt sales and gradually I got stock to sell. I kept records of what I had sold, and then went back to the bigger suppliers to show them I was being successful. They still said no, but I kept going back until finally one of them said yes. It's sometimes a matter of timing, but if you keep going you will eventually get there.'

'That's a good example of you making it sound so easy', Tom remarked smiling.

'Don't mistake me, it's not easy, but if it's what you love you make it happen. Most people give up before they get to their goal, in fact only one per cent ever get to the yes – but imagine what it feels like to be that one per cent.'

Tom's mind was racing and he had the feeling that he had just been given one of the most important pieces of information in his life. 'I think you have just given me a "magic wand" that I can really see how to use.'

Michael was delighted. 'It's not so much a magic wand as an inner core of strength that can support you all the way to the top. I like to imagine it as an iron rod engraved with the words persistence, courage, vision, desire, passion and determination and that's my backbone, that's what supports me. You have the potential for that same iron rod and all those qualities within you right now. It's simply your choice if you wish to use it or not, but imagine how invincible you would be if you did!'

Michael stood up and rolled his shoulders. 'I've been doing a lot of talking, time for a bit of exercise I think.' He smiled at Tom and moved past him into the aisle. Tom was left staring at his notes, and wondering just what his next step was going to be.

TOM'S NOTES

I BELIE(V)E — VERY, VERY PERSISTENT

- Persistence is the most hidden trait of successful entrepreneurs.
- Persistence is not will-power — it is much stronger — and is grounded in belief, passion and desire.
- Most people give up before they reach their goals — successful entrepreneurs do not.
- Entrepreneurs never accept no for an answer and are flexible and creative in the pursuit of turning a no into a yes.
- Entrepreneurs are prepared to break the rules, think differently, do whatever it takes to achieve their goals — this requires them to step outside of their comfort zone.

Chapter Seven

After Michael had walked away Tom started to review his notes. He soon realized that there was a constant thought running though his mind. He could finally glimpse what it might be like to be successful, and the germ of an idea had planted itself in his brain and was running riot. He kept returning to it, testing it and looking at it from all the angles. Could this really be the business idea he had been waiting for? He looked again at the mountain Michael had drawn in his notebook and imagined what it would be like to be standing on the pinnacle of success and what the view from the top would look like. He was vaguely aware of the other passengers around him. The woman across the aisle had long ago finished painting her nails and was now flicking through a weighty cream leather folder filled with brochures and what looked like sales material for conferences. Tom wondered if she could see the difference in him. He certainly felt different and couldn't imagine that he didn't look different too. He had got on the plane feeling anxious and preoccupied, now he was feeling energized and yet somehow more relaxed. The thought that had been chasing round his head suddenly became loud and clear and he knew he had to write it down before it escaped him. It wasn't more than a sentence or two but, using Michael's terminology that he was now feeling more familiar with, he recognized that it was truly a seed of opportunity. He hardly looked up when Michael came back down the aisle at a leisurely pace, stopping to speak to a man several seats away before making his way back. He saw Tom was deep in thought and instead of sitting down he carried on into the galley where his deep voice could be heard talking to Olivia. Tom looked again at what he had written, and then became conscious of Michael heading back to his seat. He straightened up and got his thoughts together.

'You looked totally preoccupied there. What was it you were you so involved in?' Michael made himself comfortable and Tom wondered whether to tell him how enthusiastic and energized he felt and that he had the inkling of a business idea. He hesitated, and realized he didn't want to share the idea until he had a bit more time to think about it, but he didn't want to lie to Michael either.

'I think I have got a possible business idea but, if you don't mind, I'd rather not talk about it just yet. I want it to think about it a bit longer.'

Michael nodded approvingly. 'No problem, but if you have had a great idea, then it's definitely time I shared the last principle of *I believe* with you.'

Tom was delighted to hear that, it was just what he wanted. In fact it was perfect. He held up his notebook and pen to show that he was all ready to go.

'OK. So we have got to the final "E" of *I believe* and it's the one I think most people fail to realize is equally as important to success as any of the others.'

Tom was keen to contribute. 'Let me have one final try at guessing what it is. I might be luckier this time!'

'Well, you're already showing persistence' laughed Michael. 'So go ahead'. He leaned back as Tom thought over what was left that made a successful entrepreneur.

'The first "E" was about Extending your comfort zone. The second "E" was Enjoy hard work, so I'm guessing the last "E" is for energy, enthusiasm, exceptional – am I close?'

Michael laughed out loud at the concentration on Tom's face; he obviously wanted to get this final one right.

'Yes, all those are great qualities, though not the one you will need for the final principle of *I believe*. Do you remember when I talked a while ago about my sports business?'

Tom nodded and wondered what was coming this time. He was now used to the way Michael's mind moved from subject to subject, and instead of disconcerting him it intrigued him to follow where his thoughts were going.

'The final "E" was a lesson I learned quite early on and that was to **Expect failure**.' I used to read a lot in those days, in fact everything I could get my hands on, and there was a quote that really stuck with me. It was from a politician and he said that success is going from failure to failure, without a loss of enthusiasm. In fact, I would go further and say that you need to view failure as an integral part of your overall success.'

Tom was beginning to feel confused. He was absolutely fired up to hear the last secret to being a successful entrepreneur, and here was Michael talking about failure! Well, he knew to go with it because everything else Michael had talked about made sense; there must be something he just wasn't seeing. 'I don't understand how failure is necessary to success. I can see that no one is successful all the time, but you said it was an integral part of it. How does that work?'

Michael thought for a moment of how to really make this last principle of *I believe* as clear and explicit as he could. He looked out of the plane window; outside there was nothing to see but a huge expanse of white cloud. That blank canvas helped him focus his thoughts on what he knew for most people was a topic to be avoided at all costs.

'When I had a chain of sports shops, I was looking around for another business venture, and one of the things that really attracted me was the idea of a specialist magazine devoted to running. Now running is truly my passion and has been since I was a boy. It's what got me started in business in the first place. When I looked at the market, there didn't seem to be a magazine that filled that gap so I decided this would be a great opportunity to combine business with pleasure. I researched it, got all the right people on board to write the articles, take the photographs and sell the advertising. Writers with specialist knowledge who were as keen as I was to see a magazine devoted just to runners. All the omens were good, I had checked it out, and yet within a year it was obvious that it was a failure and I had to pull the plug on it.'

Tom was intrigued. He had somehow thought that everything Michael touched turned to gold, and this was a new side of him that he was seeing. He hoped Michael wouldn't be offended, but he really wanted to know more about it.

'You seem very calm about it for something that was so close to your heart.'

'Sure, I'm calm now, though at the time I was very upset because I lost a lot of money. Also, it was the very first time I had failed at a major business venture and maybe my pride was hurt a bit too. But it turned out to be a true blessing in disguise. It's just not always obvious to you at the time, but failure is one of your greatest teachers. You have to learn from it and make sure you don't make that mistake again. Failure is how you gain experience in ways you wouldn't otherwise have access to. Look, we all make wrong decisions at some time or other, but it is essential you treat it as a learning experience, and the wisdom you get from that mistake or failure will help you to be even more successful in the future.' Michael was very sincere, Tom could hear it in his voice and he thought deeper about what he was saying as he listened to Michael elaborating on the lesson he wanted him to learn. 'What I really want you to get from my example of that failed magazine is that it is essential for any successful entrepreneur to be prepared to fail – to expect failure as part and parcel of your business. As I said, you learn more from failure than from success. Failure creates wisdom, and believe me, in my book it's not the person who fails that is the problem. *I believe* that it's those people who never get started on their dreams who are the real failures.'

Tom was absorbed in this, and it went against most of what he had been taught to believe. At school, at work, at home, in all those places his experience was that failure was something shameful to be quickly buried and not mentioned ever again. He had never come across it being given such a positive spin before and he was having trouble adjusting to the idea. He wanted to share this with Michael to see if he could get it straight in his head.

'I have a couple of thoughts about failure, and they are nothing like the ones you are talking about. It's always been something to be afraid of, and to avoid mentioning, certainly around my peers. They only want to hear about success.'

Michael considered this before replying in a confident, firm voice: 'That's the employee mindset talking again. When you know someone else is holding you accountable for every mistake – like your boss or your employer – then you don't want to be seen failing. When you have the millionaire mindset you realize that out of every failure an equal and powerful seed of opportunity comes, if you are willing to look for it, and those opportunities are a chance for even greater success. No successful entrepreneur has got where they are without a considerable number of failures. It's what they learn from; in fact you could argue that if you are not failing you are not trying hard enough!'

'What?' Tom was startled, and amused. 'Trying hard to fail, that's certainly a novel idea!'

'No, not trying hard to fail, just trying, over and over again. You remember about being very, very persistent? You are not going to have a one hundred per cent success rate, so you need to accept that as part of the game and use what you learn to move on. Look, entrepreneurs don't always have all the answers they need as they run their businesses – in fact they often make it up as they go along. They even get it wrong sometimes, but they keep on trying. After each failure you will know more, plan better and avoid the same mistakes. Do you see what I'm getting at?'

Tom was writing so fast he thought he didn't even want to pause to agree, so he just nodded and carried on writing. Michael watched him and waited until he had finished. 'What I'm saying is that failure is not the problem, it's how you deal with it that matters. That's what I meant with that quote I gave you a few minutes ago: "success is going from failure to failure without a loss of enthusiasm". So you can see exactly why it is essential that you stay optimistic and positive because in business what can go wrong will go wrong. It's up to you whether you see that cup as half full or half empty, but whichever you choose will make a difference to the outcome. You learn to deal with it and move on, and you can't afford to sit around worrying about it or what the consequences might be. You could end up not taking any action at all and that could be disastrous.'

Tom could see what Michael was getting at, though the remark about consequences had him thinking. He felt it was time to get some more clarification to be sure he was on the right track.

'I feel a bit uncomfortable with the idea of not being concerned about the consequences of decisions. Shouldn't you care about the outcome?'

Michael looked a bit surprised at this but could see there had been a genuine misunderstanding.

'No, I'm not saying you don't care about the consequences at all. Yes, you do need to think them through carefully, but what I'm saying is that you can't worry about them and let that prevent you making a decision and moving on. That is just you protecting your business, and to do that you might have to take a risk. Your job is to deal with problems so that whatever the business needs you put that first as your top priority. Sometimes that means taking a risk, and you are not always going to know what the outcome might be, but in some situations taking a risk can be the most sensible response to a problem.'

Tom now found he had another concept to get his head around; the idea that risk was sensible was certainly not one he had come across before and he felt it needed a bit more explanation. He could hear the stewardesses loading up the duty-free trolley and the chink of bottles and rustle of cartons made him speak quickly to get an answer before they were interrupted.

'I'm not sure I understand how a risk can be sensible. Surely the very nature of risk is the direct opposite of that?'

Michael listened, but it was clear he did not agree.

'I can see why you may think that, but risk for me is all about judgement, and judgement comes from wisdom. We just talked about how you get wisdom from your failures and that experience and knowledge helps you calculate what the actual risk is. That's what successful entrepreneurs are doing every day, and although to those outside the business it might look like they are taking huge risks; to those on the inside, who know what those decisions are based on, they see only that it is a calculated risk. Once you bring your experience and judgement into the calculation you have minimized that risk.' Michael leaned back and seemed to be searching for something else to help Tom really get it. 'Let me give you an example. Like I said, all my life I have been a runner, first as a sprinter, then middle distance and now marathons. Now you might say that for a man of my age to be running a marathon is a risk. I might not stay the course; I could get cramp, push my heart rate too high and possibly have a heart attack or collapse. Now all of those are risks. The fact is, because I have been running since my teens I'm very fit, and I know the limitations of my body. Over the years I have adjusted to my age and ability and I know I can run a marathon. I have calculated the risk and it is an acceptable one. Now, my goal is to finish that marathon; once it would have been to win it. But if I tried to do that now, then that would be an unacceptable risk. It would be pushing my body beyond its limits. That is the sum of the wisdom and experience I have gained from running other marathons and that enables me to calculate the risk. Some people still might say that it is too risky, but I don't. Now do you get it?'

Tom was thinking this through and he realized that for Michael risk meant something entirely different. Now he could see it in a more positive light but just how it was connected to the idea of failure he wasn't entirely sure. He realized he had been doodling on his notepad while Michael was speaking and that he had put the words risk and failure in two separate bubbles with arrows between them and a large question mark over them. 'So for you, risk and failure are related in some way?'

Michael thought about it for a moment. 'You know the old saying that risk brings its own reward?' Tom nodded and Michael continued. 'Well, I definitely see a connection between risk and failure. We've seen that you need judgement to take risks and you learn judgement from your failures because that's how you get vital information for the future. You could even say that the more failures you have, the better your judgement – providing you learn the lessons from it. With better judgement you can take bigger risks and get those bigger rewards. So failure isn't such a bad thing after all, is it?'

Now Tom got it, and he really liked the idea. He had never really thought about it before but as Michael had talked about failure he thought back again to his father and how he was always afraid to take a risk. He had once tried to run a small business that had started out as a favourite hobby, but it had failed within a few months. He had never talked about it or how he felt about going back to his old job. Growing up, Tom had realized it was a no-go area, that no one in the family mentioned it and it had coloured his father's whole attitude to life. He had certainly always seen the cup as half empty and with that realization, what Michael said made perfect sense. 'I have seen what happens when someone just accepts failure and doesn't try again. It has always seemed like such a huge thing to be overcome, but you are making failure seem almost ordinary.'

Michael heard something in Tom's voice that made him pause. He had struck a chord and he wanted to help Tom look at failure as something positive, not anything to be ashamed of. 'Maybe it's the word "failure" that is the problem. There is so much emotional baggage around it and you can feel shame, anger, grief, blame or a host of other things. What I suggest is you try thinking of it not as "failure", which is something huge and can be very scary, but as a mistake which is ordinary and everyday. Every one of us makes mistakes and we accept them, pay for them if necessary, and move on. If you know anyone who has never made a mistake then let me know, because I have certainly never met one!'

Tom smiled slightly. 'A mistake certainly doesn't sound as threatening as failure I must admit.'

'Exactly. If you have made a mistake you write it off to experience, cut the ties and don't waste any more time on it. Learn the lesson and take action to bring it to a close, rather than let things fester without taking action. This is important, Tom. Action to bring mistakes to a close is essential. Don't be in any doubt about it, being a successful entrepreneur carries a significant degree of stress, worry and pressure, perhaps considerably more than being an employee. When you work for someone else you can always leave and get another job. If it's your own business, then it's up to you to make sure that the business survives, come what may. You may not be able to walk away from it without losing everything you own. That is stressful, and you minimize that by being in control of all the elements involved, at least as much as you can. The more you are in control, the less room there is for things to go wrong and, so, less need to feel worried or pressured. Take the advice from a man who knows all about pressure, the way to deal with it to make fast decisions and take immediate action.'

'Even if the decisions are wrong?' suggested Tom.

'I'm sure more will be right than wrong. As I just said, we all make mistakes but it's how you deal with them that makes the difference.'

Satisfied, Tom leaned back in his seat. He now had the eight principles of *I believe*. All he had to do was put them into practice. He smiled at Michael as he started writing up his notes and felt he just had to say thank you.

'Michael, you have been really generous sharing these secrets with me. I'm so grateful to you, thanks a lot.'

Michael smiled back. 'No problem. I really hope you achieve the success you're looking for.'

Tom concentrated on writing his notes but jumped slightly when he felt Michael lightly touch his arm to get his attention.

'Oh, and by the way, that isn't quite the end. There's an extra secret you need to really make it all happen, but that can wait just a while longer!'

Delighted with the disconcerted look on Tom's face, Michael glanced over as he heard Olivia approaching with the duty-free trolley. He reached into his inside jacket pocket to get his wallet as Tom got down to finishing his notes.

TOM'S NOTES

I BELIEV(E) – EXPECT FAILURE

- You must expect failure as part of your journey of success — failure and success go hand in hand, you cannot have one without the other.
- Success is going from failure to failure without a loss of enthusiasm.
- Wisdom and judgement come from failure. You learn more from failure than success — Failure is a great teacher.
- With wisdom and judgement you can take larger calculated risks — which is essential to great success.
- Be prepared to fail, those who fail to start are the real failures
- Failure can always be turned into a positive — make sure you look for the new seeds of opportunity that come from it.
- Failure is a strong word with negative connotations — in reality you will have made a series of mistakes. Learn from those mistakes and do not make them again.
- If you're not failing, you're not trying hard enough.

Chapter Eight

Michael was in conversation with Olivia about what he might want from the duty-free trolley. They were laughing about his usual dilemma in choosing a gift, and Olivia held out a bottle of perfume which she assured him was a great choice and proceeded to wrap it up. Tom thought to himself: not only was Michael a really sharp guy but he also obviously thought about those close to him. Tom interrupted Olivia asking if he could also get one for his fiancée. Taking the duty-free bag from Olivia, Tom turned back to his notebook. He was busy getting his thoughts straight about what Michael had just told him about the 'extra secret' that he had been holding back until now. Even while he was occupied with that thought, in another part of his brain other ideas were being formulated, looked at, discarded or held on to for further development. He knew he had the beginnings of a business idea for himself that had been slowly emerging as he listened to the wisdom that Michael had passed onto him. He smiled to himself as he realized that Michael was right yet again – once you got the right idea, it wouldn't leave you alone! He glanced down at what he'd written and saw he'd underlined Michael's last words about that 'extra secret' and couldn't wait to have the whole thing complete.

Tom turned to Michael. 'You promised me an extra secret, and I know I'm being impatient, but please let's get to it now!'

'Why not?' agreed Michael. 'But before we do, I just want to make sure you have got the others safely under your belt. Run through them for me so you can then see exactly where the last one fits in. By the way, it's not really a secret but I do call it the "magic ingredient" because it is the one that binds all the others together. So, let's hear from you.' Michael gave Tom his full attention and although it felt a bit like an interview, or being called in front of the principal at school, Tom was ready to go for it. He had been reading and re-reading his notes throughout the flight so he was feeling fairly confident. To underline that fact, he closed the notebook and spoke directly from his memory and of what was on his mind.

'What I have understood, and seen from what you have told me, is that *I believe* is a great way to focus on and remember all the things that are required to be a successful entrepreneur.' Unconsciously copying Michael's earlier gesture, he ticked each item off on his fingers as he mentioned them. 'First the *I* which stands for **I believe in myself** and my ability to reach my goals, then *B* which is the **Be passionate and want it** so you totally desire those goals and are totally motivated to reach them. *E* is the willingness to **Expand my comfort zone** and really stretch myself.' He hesitated for a moment, then went on and touched his ring finger for emphasis. '*L* reminds me that **Lies and luck don't work,** and what I really remember from that is you telling me that luck is the crossroads of preparation and opportunity, not something I had thought of before.' He glanced at Michael. 'How am I doing?' Michael smiled and made a gesture for him to continue. '*I* for **Installing goals** was perhaps one of the easiest to understand because it is something I'm familiar with. What I hadn't realized was the importance of writing goals down and really paying daily attention to what you have set yourself, as it will make a big difference to what I can achieve. Now this next *E*.' He looked again at Michael to be sure he had his full attention, and Michael nodded encouragingly. 'Hard work again is something I thought I knew all about, but the concept of having to **Enjoy hard work**, well that took some thinking about. I have always worked hard, but never dreamed it could be enjoyable. I thought of it more as something you just had to do, and whether you enjoyed it or not wasn't really relevant. What you made me understand was the pleasure and excitement that can come from working on something you love, not something you are just doing for the sake of a salary.'

Michael was delighted at how Tom had taken to heart all he had told him and wanted to encourage him further. 'You are sounding like a genuine entrepreneur now Tom, so keep going!'

'Right then, I will. Moving on to the *V* of **Very, very persistent** was also an interesting one for me. Sure I know how to stick at something, but the commitment of never giving up and always trying to find a creative way to turn a no into a yes was a real learning experience. The last one though was definitely moving me into unfamiliar territory. That final *E* for **Expect failure** was a bit harder to grasp. In the end I got what you meant when you said it was truly an integral part of being successful, because you have to learn from your mistakes and be prepared to take action and move on.' He tapped the notebook with his right hand. 'I hope I haven't left anything out, but that seems to me to be the blueprint for entrepreneurial success.'

Michael was impressed. He had thought that sharing with Tom some important facts about being a successful entrepreneur would pass the time on the flight for him, but the ease and speed with which he had absorbed them and really taken them to heart convinced him that Tom was really ready to learn that last secret.

'Well, Tom, I have to say you have really impressed me. I'm delighted at how you have taken everything we have talked about, and really understood what I'm trying to pass on to you. Yes, I think it is definitely time you got that last link, my "secret ingredient" that will make a crucial difference to how successful you are. Ready for it?'

'I told you before, I can't wait. I'll just turn to a new page, and off you go.' Tom opened up his notebook and Michael told him what he wanted to know.

'The magic ingredient is all about **teamwork**. First of all you have to realize that (a) you cannot do it all by yourself. You may have terrific business ideas but it is impossible for you to be good in all areas, and to give all areas equal focus. To be a successful entrepreneur you don't need to be a great accountant or business manger. What you really need to know is point (b) that actually you get a much greater impact from a group working together than you will if you try and do it all by yourself. It's all about the synergy of teamwork, because as soon as you get two or more people focused on a problem then the magic starts to happen. Of course, each person makes a valuable contribution in their own right, but together they can do so much more. Just looking at the maths, it's two plus two equals four, but when those four people are really sparking as a team they produce a creative synergy that pushes that result from a four to a five. It's because they support, challenge and motivate each other to greater action. On your own you can get bogged down in detail; in a team you can delegate and you get feedback from others to show you where you are and to stop you from procrastinating. It's important to get things right, but it's even more important to get things going, and that's what a great team will help you to achieve.' Michael's face was alert as he talked about the qualities needed, and it was obvious that he thoroughly enjoyed working with others. Tom asked him if that was the case and Michael nodded vigorously in reply and expanded what he had just been saying.

'The real secret of lasting success is that you can't do it alone. Ultimately your success is a product of how good the people are that you surround yourself with. Remember how we talked about the moon landing? Well, Neil Armstrong was the figurehead, the entrepreneur if you like, but there was no way he could have taken that first step on the moon without an amazing team around him, in that spacecraft and back on the ground. That whole team had to have that same passionate desire and be totally motivated to get him to the moon. They were working as one unit with the same goal, and they produced the most spectacular result – they put his feet on the moon's surface. Now, he certainly wanted to be the one to get there first, but without the whole team behind him with that same desire it would not have happened. From the scientists to the switchboard operators, everyone played their part because they got inspired by the vision of America putting the first man on the moon. Once you get that kind of teamwork and support then you can get amazing, incredible results.'

'I understand you need to have support, but surely it's the entrepreneur who really gets things done?' asked Tom.

Michael shook his head decisively. 'One of the biggest mistakes entrepreneurs make is to believe they can do it all by themselves. In reality, most are not equal to it because being an entrepreneur, starting a business and taking a product or service to the marketplace is an uphill challenge and struggle. A lot of people delude themselves about their abilities, or if we go back to the principles of *I believe*, they may have some of the qualities needed but be missing a vital one. After all, the entrepreneur sees the big picture, the opportunity, that's their unique talent. But what they then need to do is get a team to help them realize that vision. When I bought a chain of sports shops, I didn't sit down and devise the marketing plan in every detail or micromanage the figures. I oversaw it, yes, but I had people that I trusted to do that, who were actually much better at marketing and financial planning than I was. To be a successful entrepreneur you have to learn how to surround yourself with people who add to your skills so that together you can produce much better results. I told you it can be an uphill struggle, so having good staff or partners will be the key to your longevity. We've talked about how important it is to be persistent, and trying to go it alone means you can get more easily discouraged. Having the support and input from others will help you keep going. Don't underestimate the power of persistence – it is absolutely crucial, and if only one per cent of approaches get to that final yes, that means ninety nine per cent have given up before they get to that point. Support and a great team means you are able to hang in there longer, right to the end.'

'I suppose in every successful business you tend to just notice the person at the top, and they certainly couldn't have got there without help, I agree with you, but surely the entrepreneur is responsible for leading and inspiring the team?' Tom was curious as it sounded as if Michael was downplaying the importance of the entrepreneur, and that just didn't fit with anything he had said so far.

'Absolutely right; the entrepreneur is responsible they are the figurehead and get all the publicity, but believe me if you take a close look at them, they have achieved their success because they have a great team around them in which they have total confidence. Having a great team is not an optional extra for me; it's a simple necessity that makes absolute business sense. It's like having a great winning football team; the manager doesn't have to be a player but they have to bring together all the different talents that make up a team and know how to bring the best out of each team member so that they win their games. It's the same for an entrepreneur; they have to assemble the right team and use all of their different skills to bring about their vision. They do not have to do it all by themselves; in fact their business will suffer if they do. Michael leaned back and looked enquiringly at Tom. 'So you think you have understood how important that "magic ingredient" is?'

While he had been listening to the words, what Tom had experienced was the real warmth and sincerity of what Michael was telling him. It felt like he had been given a terrific present, just like putting the last piece in place in a jigsaw and really seeing the whole picture for the first time. 'I have, and I can now really see my business idea taking shape. Can I run through it with you now, if that's OK?'

Over their heads the 'fasten seat belt' lights went on and they heard Olivia's voice requesting all passengers to put their seats in the upright position and fasten their seat belts to prepare for landing. Michael turned to Tom with a look of genuine curiosity and a slight challenge in his voice.

'Well, here's your first test. You will have to be succinct and clear to get your idea across before we land as you've got about five minutes!'

Tom wasn't worried. This idea had been filtering through to him the whole journey and each time he got another one of the eight principles of *I believe* it had become stronger and clearer to him. His only concern was what Michael would think of it. He might be unhappy at the idea, but the only way to find out was to go for it, so he took a deep breath.

'Everything you have told me about *I believe* has convinced me that it is a remarkable tool to help anyone who wants to become an entrepreneur. You have generously shared it with me, and as I have been writing my notes I kept thinking about how valuable it would be to pass that on to others as well. Do you agree?'

Michael looked at him keenly and after a moment's consideration he nodded his agreement, and Tom held up Michael's notebook as he continued to talk.

'Well, I would like to take these notes and turn them into a course to help others get started, and to think differently about being an entrepreneur. You've helped me move from an employee to a millionaire mindset and I want to give others that opportunity as well. Would you be willing to let me use these notes to do that?'

Michael was genuinely surprised. 'I didn't think that would be the outcome when I offered you my spare seat! But, yes, I think it is a great idea to share it with others, so what's your next step going to be?'

Tom took an even bigger breath, and hoped this came out right, and with the result he wanted. 'Well, actually I would like to ask you if you would be a mentor for me on this business idea. It would mean a lot to me, but first these notes are going in a very safe place until I can get them typed up!' Tom went to tear the pages out of the notebook, but Michael stopped him.

'No, you keep it as a symbol of how this first started, and as for being your mentor, it is very important to me that I'm able to give something back for all that I have received, so yes, you can count on me for that. You'll soon see, Tom, that all successful entrepreneurs recognize that they need to give something back for everything they have received. I'm more than happy to have shared my experience with you, and for you to use our conversation to help others be successful as well. Just remember that you too must give something back from your success, because that's the way the flow continues. The more successful entrepreneurs you meet, the more you will realize that they do want to give something back to society and you will be a part of that.

Tom was so pleased to hear that Michael would be there to support him and his mind was racing with all the ideas and plans that were just bubbling up. What Michael had given him was incredibly valuable and Tom knew that there were other millionaire entrepreneurs who would have ideas and inspiration to offer and add to what Michael had said. He started jotting names down that came to mind, famous entrepreneurs he had read about in the papers or seen interviewed on television, and soon had a shortlist. Michael watched him and asked what he was doing. Tom showed him and explained what it was.

'These are people who I want to go and talk to, to add to what you have already told me, and maybe get some different perspectives. I want to talk to as many successful entrepreneurs as I can.'

'Great idea! Give me the notebook a second.' When Tom handed it over, Michael added a couple more names. 'These last two I know well, so give them my name when you contact them. Sounds like you have the beginning of a plan here!'

Tom's face was alight with enthusiasm and energy. 'Definitely, I can't wait to get started, and I even have a name for it!'

'Let's hear it'. Michael was energized just hearing the excitement in Tom's voice.

'OK, I want to call it "Millionaire MBA". I want it to teach the things that real-life entrepreneurs know, but are not taught at business school. It will be a programme that will help people move into that millionaire mindset you talked about. I want it to be full of interviews with people like you who are willing to pass on their wisdom. I think that would be an amazing business, and something I do feel passionate about. Passing on that knowledge and helping others is something I'm sure no one else has done like this and I can't wait to get started!'

Michael knew that Tom really had got a great idea because he could see the enthusiasm and energy with which he talked about it. 'That is terrific. Now you have to keep that momentum going. Don't let all that passion and energy drift away. Anchor it with some immediate action to make it real for you. What about establishing a website?'

'Yes, I will certainly need to do that, and I need to register a name – that would make it real, wouldn't it?' Tom was practically out of his seat he was so keen to get going. Slightly surprised by his own feelings Tom looked at Michael. 'Now I know what you meant about finding your passion. I just can't wait to get started. It's all I can think about.'

'Go for it, Tom' Michael encouraged him. Seeing the way Tom was so excited and focused on his goal, Michael couldn't have been more delighted if he had come up with the idea himself.

The noise of the engines throttling back alerted both of them to the fact that they were about to land. They exchanged business cards and Tom knew that this was a great new beginning for him. Sitting next to Michael had changed his life, and he knew he would prove to be helpful well beyond the journey that they had shared together. As they were at the front of the plane, they disembarked first and as the cabin door opened and they went through the airport to passport control it was all Tom could do not to break into a run.

As they walked through together Michael stopped and shook Tom's hand. 'I need to get an internal flight now, so I will leave you here. I'm in the office Tuesday, give me a call and I will help you set up some more interviews with other entrepreneurs. I hope you will have your business plan ready by then!'

Tom returned the handshake. 'After all you have told me, I know better than to be less than one hundred per cent prepared! Thanks again, and I will call you Tuesday.' Michael strolled off and Tom headed towards the exit in a much better mood than he could ever have imagined when he first sat in seat 1B. He was ready to start his new business and he vowed to himself that one year from today he too would be a successful entrepreneur. Thinking of that seat 1B and how lucky it had been for him, he had a sudden thought and took out the notebook Michael had given him. He stepped aside from the press of people who were hurrying past him to get to the passport control area and found a blank page. He wrote a large, bold, note to himself and put an asterisk in front of it and grinned as he saw the words 'Be the successful entrepreneur who always travels in seat 1A!' on the page. Tucking the notebook back into his jacket pocket he walked out looking for an internet terminal so he could register his new business. Spotting the internet café he grinned and walked towards his new life.

TOM'S NOTES

THE 'MAGIC INGREDIENT'

- Entrepreneurs surround themselves with great people and build a fantastic team of people who complement their own skills.
- Never think you can do it all alone — you can't.
- Teams create synergy: two plus two equals five when you have a good team.
- The team must share your passion, belief and desire — it is your job to inspire them.
- Great entrepreneurs have great mentors — find yourself a mentor.
- Success comes from action — you must anchor your words and enthusiasm with action. Build on each step with more action. Do not procrastinate.
- Give something back for your own success — what you give out you will receive back one thousand times over.
- Always carry a notebook with you — you never know who you are going to meet or what ideas you will need to capture.
- Always travel in seat 1A.

Millionaire MBA – a true story

Although the character of Tom is fictional, his idea for creating a mentoring course for entrepreneurs is very real.

Before writing *Millionaire Upgrade*, the author, Richard Parkes Cordock wanted to find out first hand from real-life self-made millionaires what made them so successful.

Armed with the belief that this knowledge could be shared to the benefit of many, Richard interviewed 50 self-made millionaires and business experts, discovering the common traits and characteristics among them.

The culmination of his work is the highly acclaimed *Millionaire MBA™ Business Mentoring Programme*. Over 8-weeks, real-life entrepreneurs share their proven strategies and mentor you to success in your own business.

Millionaire MBA includes 3 flexible learning formats:

1. 25 hours of mentoring from real-life entrepreneurs.
Available on audio or MP3 CD. Choose which format works best for you.

2. 100 page workbook.
Practical, hands-on exercises to bring the whole programme together helping you apply the knowledge and learning to your own circumstances.

3. 20 days of audio transcripts.
As well as listening to *Millionaire MBA™* whilst you travel, exercise or relax – you can read the full text version of the programme with over **500 pages** of high-quality audio transcripts.

Visit online at
www.millionairemba.com

www.millionairemba.com

**Download your FREE
Podcast & Entrepreneur Interviews**

Discover additional insights
from the real-life entrepreneurs
whose contributions made
this book happen and read
the original story of Sir Richard Branson
and the upgraded passenger:

www.millionairemba.com/upgrade

Index

action 23–4, 48, 55
anxiety 3–4

business idea 24, 91, 92, 105, 111,
    112–16

challenges 21, 77
change 9, 48
choice 17, 71–2
comfort zone
    extending 36–8
    facts 39
    fear of moving out of 31, 34–5
    feeling discomfort 32–3
    remaining in 31
    risk-taking 31
    waiting for right moment 29–30
commitment 47–8, 56
control 9
creating what you need to create 17

decision-making 48, 94, 97, 101
desire 21, 81, 82, 83, 84
doing things you would rather not do 8
doing things your own way 17
dreams 17–18, 59, 60

education 11, 12, 13
entrepreneurs 11–12
    key characteristics 20–1
    motivation 16
    passion more than money 16, 17

successful 23, 33, 69, 98

failure 9
    acceptance of 33–4, 96, 100
    and creation of wisdom 95
    dealing with 96–7, 101
    expectations of 93–101
    as great teacher 94
    helpful facts 102
    as learning experience 94–6, 100
    as a mistake 100–1
    as positive experience 99
focus 3, 20, 84, 115
    on goals 59, 61–2, 69
    letting slip 14–15
    vision and desire 82
forward planning 5–6
freedom 17
frustration 3–4, 9
    with work 10–11, 18–19

goals 115
    achieving 47, 60–2, 84
    business 55
    clearly defined 55–6, 58, 84
    conceive it, achieve it 58
    as dreams with deadlines 59
    focus on 59, 61–2, 69
    helpful facts 63
    pay attention to 55
    as permanent feature 54–5
    personal 55, 56, 71